The New Middle Ages

The New Middle Ages is a series dedicated to pluridisciplinary studies of medieval cultures, with particular emphasis on recuperating women's history and on feminist and gender analyses. This peer-reviewed series includes both scholarly monographs and essay collections.

More information about this series at
http://www.palgrave.com/gp/series/14239

W. Mark Ormrod

Women and Parliament in Later Medieval England

palgrave
macmillan

W. Mark Ormrod
York, UK

The New Middle Ages
ISBN 978-3-030-45219-3 ISBN 978-3-030-45220-9 (eBook)
https://doi.org/10.1007/978-3-030-45220-9

Cover illustration: Artmedia / Alamy Stock Photo
Cover design by eStudio Calamar

This Palgrave Macmillan imprint is published by the registered company Springer Nature Switzerland AG.
The registered company address is: Gewerbestrasse 11, 6330 Cham, Switzerland

For Rebecca and Helen

Preface

This study of *Women and Parliament in Later Medieval England* began life as a long article and turned rapidly into a short book. I am extremely grateful to Megan Laddusaw and Allie Troyanos for picking up my ideas for a Palgrave Pivot with such alacrity, and to Bonnie Wheeler, the editor of 'The New Middle Ages' series, for her support of the project's inclusion in the series list.

I record my thanks to Cordelia Beattie, Gwilym Dodd, Judith Frost, Helen Lacey, Amanda McVitty and Anthony Musson for their helpful comments on earlier drafts of this study, to Jonathan Mackman and Shelagh Sneddon for expert readings of documents, and to Shelagh Sneddon for her work on the index and general checking of the text. The two anonymous readers for the press sent meticulous notes and provided generously of their own knowledge, to the general benefit of my text.

At home I have, as always, benefited from the support of Richard Dobson and our two families. This book is for my nieces, Rebecca Ormrod and Helen Ormrod, to mark their own distinctive and courageous pursuit of womanhood.

York, UK
January 2020

Contents

Abbreviations[1]

CCR	*Calendar of the Close Rolls Preserved in the Public Record Office, Henry III–Henry VII*, 61 vols (London: His/Her Majesty's Stationery Office, 1892–1963).
CFR	*Calendar of the Fine Rolls Preserved in the Public Record Office, Edward I–Henry VII*, 22 vols (London: His/Her Majesty's Stationery Office, 1911–1962).
CIM	*Calendar of Inquisitions Miscellaneous, 1219–1485*, 8 vols (London/Woodbridge: His/Her Majesty's Stationery Office/Boydell, 1916–2003).
CIPM	*Calendar of Inquisitions Post Mortem, Henry III–Henry V*, 20 vols (London: His/Her Majesty's Stationery Office, 1904–1995).
CPR	*Calendar of the Patent Rolls Preserved in the Public Record Office, Henry III–Henry VII*, 54 vols (London: His/Her Majesty's Stationery Office, 1891–1916).
PROME	Paul Brand, Seymour Phillips, W. Mark Ormrod, Geoffrey Martin, Chris Given-Wilson, Anne Curry and Rosemary Horrox, eds, *The Parliament Rolls of Medieval England*, 16 vols (Woodbridge: Boydell, 2005).
RP	J. Strachey, ed., *Rotuli Parliamentorum*, 6 vols (London: Record Commission, 1767–1777).
RPHI	H. G. Richardson and G. O. Sayles, eds, *Rotuli Parliamentorum Anglie Hactenus Inediti*, Camden Society 3rd ser. 51 (London, 1935).
SR	John Raithby, ed., *The Statutes of the Realm*, 11 vols (London: Record Commission, 1810–1828).

Note

1. All unpublished documents are in Kew, The National Archives of the United Kingdom. All references to the parliament rolls are given in three formats: the original document in the National Archives; the eighteenth-century edition of *Rotuli Parliamentorum*; and the modern English version (with the translations used here) in the print version of *The Parliament Rolls of Medieval England*. The electronic version of *The Parliament Rolls of Medieval England* (CD-ROM; Leicester, 2004) is not easily accessible to many readers, but those with access to it can check the references by ensuring that the texts of the relevant rolls are switched to 'page' mode, which reveals the original pagination of *Rotuli Parliamentorum*.

CHAPTER 1

Introduction: Debates and Sources

Abstract The history of Parliament is almost always written as the history of men, and especially for the Middle Ages when women were so often excluded, formally or informally, from political institutions. Yet there was a long history during the later medieval period of women (like men) petitioning the Crown in Parliament for the redress of grievances. The best evidence for this comes from the first 7910 petitions in the National Archives series SC 8, whose parliamentary provenance is well established. Some 12% of this sample comprises petitions by women, acting either as *femme sole* (that is, independently) or in conjunction with husbands, as well as smaller numbers of petitions from female collectives (mainly houses of nuns). This book offers a sustained analysis of this material, set within a number of modern theoretical positions on medieval women, especially the question of women's power and agency.

Keywords Agency • Gender • Parliament • Petitions • Power • Women

W. M. Ormrod, *Women and Parliament in Later Medieval England*, The New Middle Ages,
https://doi.org/10.1007/978-3-030-45220-9_1

The History of Parliament

The year 2018 was the centenary of the Representation of the People Act 1918, by which some women over the age of thirty were permitted to vote, for the first time, in elections to the British Parliament. The anniversary was marked with a good deal of activity both in Parliament itself and in academic circles, which evaluated and celebrated the work of suffragists, suffragettes and male politicians in bringing about the great sea-change in women's role in politics over the course of the twentieth century. Much less attention was given to the fact that women had been participants in the wider political culture of Parliament for a long time before 1918. In an important article published in 2019, Sarah Richardson has drawn attention to the role of women as wives and servants in the Palace of Westminster before and after the great fire of 1834. In particular, she has elucidated women's access to the Commons, before 1834 via the 'Ventilator' air shaft running out of the Commons Chamber and after 1852 in the Ladies' Gallery of the (then newly built) House of Commons.[1] Richardson's study naturally prompts the medievalist to the question: What role did women play in the life of Parliament during the earliest centuries of the institution's existence? This study aims to address that question in relation to the late thirteenth, fourteenth and fifteenth centuries.

The English Parliament had many antecedents stretching back into the pre-Conquest and Norman eras, but it was in the thirteenth century that a recognisable institution with the actual name of Parliament—from the Latin and French terms for 'talking' or 'debating'—first emerged.[2] Its functions, as they developed through the reigns of Henry III, Edward I and Edward II, were three-fold: to discuss and advise the king on the great affairs of state, such as the making of new laws and the pursuit of foreign policy; to provide a forum in which the king's subjects could approach him directly for the redress of their individual grievances, expressed in the form of 'private' petitions; and to obtain formal consent for the levying of extraordinary taxes needed for the prosecution of war. In order to be accepted, private petitions had to meet certain criteria, the most important of which was that the matter in hand could not be dealt with adequately by the common law courts but needed to be resolved either by the dispensation of the king's grace or by the delegation of the matter to a special judicial commission of oyer and terminer (literally 'to hear and determine').

Early in Edward III's reign, the composition of Parliament settled down into the characteristic two orders or, as they were often later known, 'houses', the Lords and the Commons. The former was a group of fifty to a hundred titled nobles and barons who were summoned to Parliament in their own right as the successors to the members of older Great Councils. The Commons was made up of two groups: the knights of the shires, who were elected in the county courts by the substantial freeholders of the relevant counties; and the citizens and burgesses, who were chosen by the local elites in up to a hundred self-governing cities and towns. The knights of the shires, numbering seventy or so men (two from each county) tended to be drawn from landed society below the ranks of the Lords, often referred to today as the gentry. The citizens and burgesses, who numbered around a hundred and fifty (again, two from each constituency), were normally from mercantile stock. In the fifteenth century, some of the parliamentary boroughs preferred to elect members of the gentry to represent them in Parliament, and throughout the later Middle Ages the landed interest always tended to prevail, though merchants' voices were sometimes loudly expressed in the common petitions. There were also potentially a hundred and fifty clerical proctors, representing the diocesan clergy and cathedral chapters; although we know the names of these men, they are almost entirely invisible in the records of Parliament, and it remains uncertain whether they attended or what role they had.

There was a perennial problem about attendance among the lay members, too: a number of the Lords, and even some of those elected to the Commons and in receipt of expenses from their constituencies, did not bother to turn up at certain Parliaments over the fourteenth and fifteenth centuries. Sometimes this was to do with the inconvenience of the venue. In its earlier years, Parliament met wherever the king planned to be at the allotted time: the use of the northern capital of York as a frequent meeting-place for Parliament from the 1290s to the 1330s reflected the preoccupation of successive monarchs with war against the Scots. Gradually, however, Westminster prevailed, though other places such as Gloucester, Cambridge, Leicester and Coventry were used as 'one-offs' for sessions of Parliament in the later fourteenth and fifteenth centuries.

It was in Edward III's time that Parliament gained exclusive control not only over the direct taxes granted in time of war but also over the range of subsidies on exports and imports which, together with the older customs duties levied in the ports, represented by far the largest single element in the Crown's fiscal armoury. Parliament found a number of ways to link the granting of taxation with the redress of grievances expressed in so-called 'common' petitions. Thus, from the middle of the fourteenth century the great majority of royal statutes represented measures that had been agreed in Parliament by the king with the consent of the Lords and Commons.

Parliament did not sit permanently—some medieval historians have preferred to regard it as an 'occasion' rather than an institution—and the frequency of assemblies varied. Under Edward I, it was common to hold three Parliaments a year; under Edward III, it was more usual to have just one; and by the time of Henry VI and Edward IV, several years could sometimes go by without any Parliaments being summoned. The decline in frequency partly accounts for the dropping away of the individual or 'private' petitions that had been so important an element of parliamentary business under Edward I and Edward II. The growth in the equitable jurisdiction of the court of Chancery during the fourteenth century was in part a response to the need of petitioners to have regular access to a tribunal outside and beyond the common law.[3] But with the decline in the number of Parliaments went a concomitant increase in the amount of public business done there. Whereas individual Parliaments under Edward I had often met for just a week or two, by the fifteenth century they were often in session for several months, and might be prorogued and reconvened multiple times.

When it was in session, then, Parliament as a body comprised up to a hundred members of the Lords and around two hundred and fifty members of the Commons, not to mention the proctors of the clergy and the various royal officials in attendance *ex officio* or as providers of administrative support. All of these were men: whereas women have been identified as holding some public offices, such as sheriff, under exceptional circumstances during the later Middle Ages, no-one has ever discovered a woman summoned in her own right to the Lords or returned by the counties or towns to the Commons.[4] It is reasonable to suppose that women were sometimes present on the fringes of Parliament. The wives of at least some parliamentarians may have accompanied their husbands to the venue for assembly and spent part of their time there observing the debates held in the Lords' and Commons' chambers, either first-hand or, more probably, second-hand via men's oral summaries. The social side of Parliament is poorly studied, however, and we know very little about whether women ever joined even in the ceremonial aspects of such political assemblies.[5] In this respect, the records are remarkably unyielding as to the possible presence of women at the various meeting-places of Parliament during the later Middle Ages.

It is easy and tempting to take silence as absence, and to suppose that women were not present at all during sessions of Parliament. One case helps typify such a view. Everard Digby of Stoke Dry (Rutland), esquire, was chosen as knight of the shire, first for Huntingdonshire and later for the county of Rutland, on seven occasions between 1439 and 1459.[6] At one of his parliamentary attendances, most likely the post-Easter sessions of 1449 or 1450, Digby submitted a petition complaining of various wrongs done to him by John Cheseldene, esquire, of Uppingham. In particular, Digby reported that, while he had been in London and occupied in the business of Parliament, Cheseldene's men had come to his house in the manner of war and had shot arrows at his wife, Agnes, and their servants.[7] Except for the detail about the plaintiff's absence on the king's business in Parliament, the petition stands as one of hundreds, if not thousands, that were received by the English Crown over the course of the late thirteenth to the late fifteenth century. Had any of the property held by Everard come to him by right of Agnes, the petition would have been made in their joint names. In this case, however, as in so many others, the plaintiff's wife took a strictly subordinate role: an important part of the case made against the defendant, she remains nonetheless mute in the surviving record, her own account of the affray being channelled entirely by her husband.

The Digby-Cheseldene quarrel therefore epitomises some generally accepted truisms about the role of women in medieval public life. Left at home while their husbands went about the business of the town, the county and the realm, married women might take on additional responsibilities for the household and estates in the absence of their menfolk. However, so long as they remained under the legal form of coverture—that is, quite literally were 'covered' by their husbands—they were unable to assert an independent status at law and thus to prosecute their own business in any court, including Parliament. Noble, gentry and other free women bound in coverture retained certain rights, not least because of the practice of devolving part of the husband and wife's shared estate to the wife as dower, to provide her with her own income during her husband's life.[8] However, even when they were unmarried or widowed, women's ability to participate in public affairs was severely circumscribed by their exclusion from the formal bodies that determined so much of the business of political life: the civic and county courts, as well as Parliament itself.[9] As one female petitioner to Parliament, Christina de Mareys, put it in 1305, women should not have letters of protection from the Chancery covering them against false prosecutions in the courts because they could not provide public service to the king, the only proper grounds on which such protections ought to be issued.[10] Nor did Parliament admit the idea that women of very high status might be permitted to have some formal involvement within the institution. In 1425 it was stated quite starkly in Parliament that Edward III's cousin, Margaret Marshal (d. 1399), in spite of being acknowledged as countess and later duchess of Norfolk in her own right, was a noble person 'to whom no place in parlement might apperteyne, by cause she was a woman'.[11]

The present study arises from a perceived need to re-assess the place that women were accorded, or that they asserted, in the business of Parliament during the period from the reign of Edward I to that of Henry VII. In addressing the work of Parliament during these first centuries of its existence, historians commonly draw a basic distinction between the common business of the realm and the private business of the corporate bodies and individuals who brought their grievances for redress.[12] Such a distinction was explicitly recognised by the anonymous author of the *Modus tenendi parliamentum*, a treatise on Parliament written most likely in the early 1320s. The *Modus* regarded it as imperative that Parliament should prioritise the great affairs of the realm, treating private complaints only secondarily and on a first-come, first-served basis.[13] This bold statement was, however, an expression more of hope than of reality. The discussions of broader themes about law and government that took place in Parliament were not infrequently provoked by individual cases.[14] For example, a common petition dating from one of the Parliaments held between 1319 and 1325 addressed the right of heirs to recover lands which they should have inherited from their mothers but which had been alienated by their fathers. When the Crown responded, it specifically cited an earlier discussion of the issue prompted by a private petition registered at the Lincoln Parliament of 1316.[15] Furthermore, by the later fourteenth century, as private petitions tended to be squeezed out by the pressure of major issues, private parties still found ways of having their business addressed in Parliament by lobbying the Commons for their complaints to be included in the schedule of common petitions normally submitted to the king and Council in each assembly.[16] Gwilym Dodd and Simon Payling, the only historians thus far explicitly to address the question of women's role in the later medieval Parliament, have approached the topic solely in terms of the individual supplications of women for the remedy and advancement of their personal circumstances and interests.[17] However, women's issues, as we may hazard to call the clusters of business that emerge from those private and common petitions either submitted by women or claiming in some way to address their interests, happen to demonstrate particularly well the continuum between private causes and public debates on which Parliament based its considerations of what was, and was not, for the common good.

Accordingly, in what follows, the traditional distinction between 'private' and 'public' aspects of parliamentary business is rejected in preference for a more generalised and holistic approach to the role and treatment of women in and by Parliament. This is intended to highlight the problem of treating women's history simply in terms of the binary between the private sphere of the household and the public sphere of business, law and politics. Contrary to Christina de Mareys' restricted world view, there is every sign that a proportion of women—mainly, but not exclusively, from the elite and middle ranks of society—saw Parliament as a place where they could gain much more visibility and satisfaction for their causes than they might in the common law courts, and where the interests of their gender might be advanced.

Sources and Method

Before we proceed to such an analysis, it is necessary to make some preliminary comments about sources. There are three principal types of primary evidence on which this study depends. First are the parliament rolls, the official records of proceedings in Parliament, which summarise the formal resolution of each assembly and (at least from the 1340s onwards) contain full transcriptions of the common petitions and the Crown's answers to them. Secondly, we can take into account unofficial narratives of events in certain Parliaments, sometimes written by or under the influence of eyewitnesses, and which are preserved in contemporary tracts and chronicles. These sometimes flesh out the more unusual and dramatic episodes in parliamentary history and provide detail that the clerks of Parliament deliberately or accidentally omitted from the parliament rolls. Finally, there are the significant numbers of extant private petitions on which we can base both quantitative and qualitative analyses of the business brought to Parliament by female supplicants.

In this last respect, the present study relies principally on a survey of the first 7910 documents in the longer National Archives series SC 8 (Ancient Petitions). This sub-group comprises the contents of a set of files that survived until the nineteenth century under the label 'Parliamentary Petitions', and whose parliamentary provenance is the strongest.[18] The remaining *c.* 10,000 documents in the Ancient Petitions are much more diverse in terms of the officeholder and/or institution before which they were presented.[19] However, Gwilym Dodd has demonstrated that a significant proportion of the 2279 documents that follow on immediately after the 'Parliamentary Petitions' in the file sequence of the Ancient Petitions were indeed presented in Parliament; and there are others scattered more randomly through the rest of the series that can also be proved from internal evidence or other contextual sources to have been submitted in Parliament. Throughout this study, this wider range of documents is used selectively to provide additional information and examples of important features of women's petitions. The core of the analysis, however, rests on the 7910 documents derived from the original files of 'Parliamentary Petitions'.

Within this discrete body of material, I have located a total of 921 petitions in which women appear as petitioners, either alone, or in conjunction with a husband, or very occasionally with other parties. These petitions

Table 1.1 Women's petitions among the 'Parliamentary Petitions' in the Ancient Petitions

Category	*Number*	*Percentage of the sample (7910 documents)*
Queens as petitioners	6	0.1%
Women petitioning in their own right (*femmes soles*)	150	1.9%
Women petitioning as daughters of named fathers (*femmes soles*)	77	1.0%
Women petitioning jointly with their husbands	262	3.3%
Women petitioning as widows (*femmes soles*)	354	4.5%
Female religious houses[a]	77	1.0%
Total	**926**	**11.7%**

[a]This category includes all female religious attached to the monastic and mendicant orders, including the mixed order of the Gilbertines. In this instance, it was the house, not the nun, which was normally the petitioner (see below, 64–66). Hospitals sometimes petitioned in the name of the 'master and brothers' of the given house, and sometimes in the name of the '[master,] brethren and sisters'. Where sisters are mentioned in the address clause (9 instances within the sample) I have included them in the sub-total of female religious houses

break down into a number of readily recognisable categories, represented in Table 1.1.

It becomes immediately apparent from these data that women were at a disadvantage in terms of their ability to petition in Parliament: given that they were as numerous (if not more so) as men in later medieval England, the fact that women petitioned in only just under 12% of the instances represented by the contents of the 'Parliamentary Petitions' shows just how far the petitioning system was skewed in favour of men.[20] The fact that women were almost always denied direct involvement in public institutions, coupled with the situation whereby married women were considered by the law to be covered by their husbands, meant that the number of women petitioners, and the circumstances under which women tended to petition, were heavily circumscribed.

The 'Parliamentary Petitions' within the series 'Ancient Petitions' are not the only recourse for evidence of women petitioners to Parliament in the later Middle Ages. The medieval parliament rolls, published as *Rotuli Parliamentorum* in the late eighteenth century and as *The Parliament Rolls of Medieval England* in the early twenty-first century, also included private petitions, especially in the early years of Parliament under Edward I and Edward II and then again, increasingly, after the end of the fourteenth century. In some cases these can be traced back to originals in the series 'Ancient Petitions'; in other instances, however, the originals do not survive. *Rotuli Parliamentorum* also includes private petitions not on the parliament roll but which had been transcribed at an earlier date from the original files of parliamentary petitions then still in existence. In some of these cases, the originals are no longer extant, so the eighteenth-century edition is used as the authority. In this study, all three categories of petitions—originals in the 'Ancient Petitions', transcriptions onto the parliament rolls, and editions of lost petitions in *Rotuli Parliamentorum*, are employed.

Petitions of all kinds were, on the whole, written by people with some expertise in formal documentation and points of law. These included the scriveners who operated in many late medieval English towns as well as the attorneys, people who made a living from representing plaintiffs in the courts. In some cases, petitions were taken to Parliament in bundles collected by the relevant members of the Commons. In other cases, petitioners relied on the expert services of clerks employed by the City of London, in which case they might send forward their complaint in oral form via a messenger or attorney. All of this preparation work was done, then, by men. It is therefore evident, and vitally important to acknowledge, that the texts of the documents at our disposal do not provide the unmediated voices of women. Many of the rhetorical phrases and legal usages deployed in such petitions were a matter of form, and cannot be read as unique to any female (or, indeed, male) petitioner. It is still possible, however, to gain glimpses of the plaintiff's own viewpoint through the descriptions of the wrongs perpetrated by the defendant, the incidental details provided, and, in a small number of cases, the use of reported speech and of the first-person singular. (Petitions were conventionally written in the third person.)[21]

The great majority of petitions in the three categories described above date from the first century of Parliament's existence, between the reigns of Edward I and Richard II.[22] Edward I actively encouraged the use of Parliament as a place where his free subjects could petition for remedy of wrongs. This was initially a very popular route. At the end of the thirteenth century, Parliament normally met three times a year, providing ample opportunity for the submission of petitions. Petitioning was also cheap: by comparison with the hierarchy of writs that had to be purchased from the Chancery to institute process in the common law courts, petitioners had only to find the fee for writing the initial petition and to ensure its passage to the place where Parliament was to meet. By the end of Edward II's reign, however, there were regular complaints that the resulting deluge of cases could not be processed during the short periods when Parliament actually sat. As a result, from Edward III's time, and more especially in the fifteenth century, those seeking alternative routes to justice outside the jurisdiction of the common law turned their attention increasingly to other prerogative courts that dispensed the king's grace. The most important of these was the court of Chancery, which emerged over the later fourteenth and fifteenth centuries as a place where plaintiffs could initiate procedure by petition. (These petitions survive in the National Archives series C 1.) The rise of the court of Chancery, presided over by the chancellor, proceeded apace, much facilitated by the convention that it, unlike the common law courts and Parliament, was always open for business—even during the three- to four-month period in the summer when the other regular judicial and financial offices at Westminster shut down.[23] Since Parliament itself met much less frequently in the fifteenth century than before, those who did continue to petition there did so principally in order to get their petitions taken up by the Commons and submitted to the Crown as common petitions, with the possibility of remedy being provided in statutory form. This, in turn, meant that those who continued to submit private petitions in Parliament were of a relatively high social status: the pleas of peasant women, which one finds in significant numbers in the time of Edward I, were no longer a feature of Parliament under Henry VI.

It is noticeable from the texts of the sample of documents set out in Table 1.1 that women petitioning in Parliament did not explicitly assert the status of independent woman. In other legal and fiscal records, unmarried adult women began after the Statute of Additions of 1413 to be given the designation *femme sole*, rendered into the Middle English vernacular as 'single woman'. In the case of urban society, *femme sole* status was sometimes licensed by the relevant borough court; but in most cases it was simply assumed on the basis that the woman was unmarried or widowed.[24] The great majority of the 150 cases of single women in the sample of 'Parliamentary Petitions' used here are datable before 1413, but it is still striking that the status was never asserted explicitly with the names of the female petitioners in the formal address clauses after this date. In fact, there are only two instances where *femme sole* status is mentioned within the substance of late fourteenth-century petitions, and both of these turn out to be exceptional cases, discussed in Chaps. 2 and 4.[25] It thus becomes evident that the majority of instances in which laywomen participated in the petitioning process in Parliament occurred in two discreet stages of the life-cycle: during marriage, when for various reasons it was necessary formally to include the female partner as co-petitioner alongside her husband; and (more so) during widowhood, when women enjoyed not only the legal status of *femme sole* but also a significant degree of socially constructed independence from their sons and other male relatives.[26]

In these senses, the general pattern of petitioning to Parliament conforms to what is already understood about the occasions and volume of women's causes in other late medieval courts.[27] Timothy S. Haskett, surveying a sample of 6850 petitions to the court of Chancery over the period 1417–1532, found that 21% of petitioners to Chancery were women (including married women petitioning with their husbands).[28] It is interesting in this respect that Emma Hawkes has suggested, albeit on the basis of a very limited sample, that women were three times more likely to prosecute a case to Chancery in the fifteenth century than in one of the central common law courts; her hypothesis about the greater opportunities perceived to be offered to women in Chancery evidently holds true, too, for Parliament in the fourteenth century.[29] Recently, Cordelia Beattie has elucidated some of the reasons why women were drawn to the Chancery as a place of recourse, emphasising that they did not thereby assume that this was the only place where litigation might be effective, but stressing the ability of the chancellor to cut through the morass of process in other jurisdictions—including manorial, borough and ecclesiastical courts—and to have the case sent back there for speedy delivery.[30]

Petitioning in Parliament also offered the possibility of direct access to the king. Although many supplications of a more routine nature were dealt with by the special committees of spiritual and lay peers appointed in each Parliament as triers of petitions, the most intractable cases, and the ones that could only be determined by the application of royal grace, were reserved for special hearings before the king and Council.[31] Petitioning in Parliament continued to be seen as an effective means of accessing direct justice from the monarch; and women petitioners—with the assistance of the men who actually composed and wrote the relevant documentation—were, as we shall see, adept at reminding the king of his responsibilities in addressing their circumstances as the self-consciously more vulnerable gender.[32]

Women, Power and Agency

The ensuing analysis aims to treat the evidence in such a way as to interrogate the assumptions so far made about the manner in which Parliament's workings allowed the participation of women. Unlike previous studies, this book does not confine itself to women as petitioners—though inevitably, a good deal of the evidence is drawn from women's petitions in the 'Parliamentary Petitions' section of the Ancient Petitions and other parts of that series. In so doing, it aims to make three specific contributions to the history of medieval women.

First, in as far as is possible, the study attempts to provide a proper context in which to discuss women's role in medieval political life, both as pursuers and champions of their rights and sometimes as the pawns and victims of a patriarchal system. It is useful to think about women's position *vis-à-vis* Parliament in the Middle Ages in terms of a distinction that has become common (especially in studies of queenship) between authority and power, where authority, invested almost always in men, was 'the publicly recognised right to give direction and expect compliance' and power, exercised by both men and women at various social levels, was 'the ability to get people to do things or to make things happen, involving pressure, influence, [and] persuasion'.[33] Women appear in the records of Parliament not just in the prosecution of their own private petitions but as the subjects of a range of public debates, by men, on what we refer to here as 'women's issues'. By demonstrating that women themselves challenged the status quo and sought remedies on such matters outside the workings of the common law, we can see how they used their power as petitioners to push forward views that were variously reflected, or confounded, in the making of new legislation. The two particular topics on which this analysis is based are the law of dower and the law of rape, where we will witness (in Chaps. 6 and 7) the coming together, in creative or destructive tension, of women's and men's vantage points as they played out in private petitions, common petitions, and statutory reforms.

Secondly, this study aims explicitly to profile women's petitions presented in Parliament as a valuable source of life-writing in the later Middle Ages. Recently, the debate on authority and power has evolved into the study of agency, and the ability of royal, aristocratic, gentle, and working women pro-actively to pursue their own agendas and rights in the courts. This involves the deconstruction of the patriarchal discourses prevalent in the records in order to reveal the authentic voice of the female protagonist, as she told her own story in a way that she believed would catch the attention of law-makers and thus effect a resolution to her complaint.[34] Parliamentary petitions offer a particularly rich vein of material in this respect. It is true, as we have noted, that these were written to an accepted formula and followed some of the same conventions as the common law courts—especially those that required a claim of physical violence in order that the case be accepted for prosecution.[35] However, female (and male) petitioners in Parliament not infrequently broke out of these bounds to add considerably more detail about the predicaments in which they found themselves, and these narratives often have a sense of personal immediacy such as to suggest that the supplicant's words were supplied verbatim to the clerk responsible for writing the document. In a very few cases, as we shall see in Chaps. 2 and 9, female petitioners in Parliament even went so far as to use the first-person address in their petitions, thus breaking the convention of third-person writing in legal documents and effectively turning their petitions into personal letters to the king. One of the tantalising things about using the Ancient Petitions is that the moments that they represented in the lives of the plaintiffs cannot often be expanded in order to work out entirely what happened before, or after, the submission of the petition. By providing, wherever possible and however briefly, something of the social and political contexts in which women connected with Parliament, we can at least hope to add something to the field of letter- and life-writing, which is so important for the scholarly pursuit of female self-consciousness and individualism in pre-modern England.[36]

Thirdly and finally, this book aims to contribute to feminist theory by setting the individual experiences of women in Parliament within the wider social, legal and political context of the day. The first wave of feminist scholarship, from the 1960s to the 1980s, tended to emphasise the binary of the public and the private spheres and to cast women as emphatically contained and controlled by the latter space.[37] This led, in turn, to an examination of the roles of their menfolk, whether fathers, husbands, brothers or sons, in the maintenance of patriarchy. An important paradigm in this respect was the short but influential 1974 essay by Jo Ann McNamara and Suzanne Fonay Wemple, which argued that the growth of justice and bureaucracy and the consequent decline of the royal household as the principal agency of government during the eleventh and twelfth centuries led to a decline in the effective power that women were able to wield in later medieval Europe.[38]

Since the 1990s, however, women's historians have questioned the binary of public and private and sought to place women as active or passive participants in the supposed men's world of legal proceedings and political debates. Among the landmarks in this respect were the publications in 1988 and 2003 of two volumes of essays, both edited by Mary C. Erler and Maryanne Kowaleski, titled *Women and Power in the Middle Ages* and *Gendering the Master Narrative: Women and Power in the Middle Ages*.[39] Erler and Kowaleski sought explicitly 'to provide some fresh ways of analyzing women's agency ([for example,] to complexify the use of the public/private dichotomy) and to suggest some fresh forms in which female influence could be seen (through social networks instead of patronage, or family membership as opposed to accounts of "great women")'.[40] Meanwhile, in 1995, Jennifer Carpenter and Sally-Beth McLean had edited *Power of the Weak*, whose contributors focused again on destabilising the public/private binary.[41] These were followed in 2006 by Judith M. Bennett's contribution to theory in medieval studies, *History Matters*, which included an important essay on 'Patriarchal Equilibrium'. Bennett argued that patriarchy is 'contingent, constructed, and subject to change', and questioned the passivity of women in the face of male domination by pointing out that, in past cultures, 'women have … colluded in, undermined, and survived patriarchy'.[42] Most recently, in 2019, Heather Tanner has edited another series of essays titled *Medieval Elite Women and the Exercise of Power*. Tanner and her contributors argue against the notion that elite women's power declined in the later Middle Ages and rebuff the notion that any example of female agency is simply an exception to a dominant rule.[43] As a result of these studies, we now have a rich vein of empirical evidence and theoretical approaches that allow for a more nuanced account of the place of women in the networks of power that operated in later medieval England.

Notes

1. Richardson, 'Parliament as Viewed through a Woman's Eyes'.
2. Maddicott, *Origins of the English Parliament*. For what follows, see also McKisack, *Parliamentary Representation of the English Boroughs*; Powell and Wallis, *House of Lords*; Fryde and Miller, eds, *Historical Studies*; Harriss, *King, Parliament and Public Finance*; Edwards, *Second Century*; Roskell, Clark and Rawcliffe, *House of Commons*; Dodd, *Justice and Grace*; and Bradford and McHardy, eds, *Proctors for Parliament*.
3. See below, 10.
4. Wilkinson, 'Women in English Local Government'.
5. A starting point is provided by Cooper and Gaunt, 'Architecture and Politics'.
6. Wedgwood, *History of Parliament*, 273.
7. SC 8/105/5244.
8. Rowena E. Archer, '"How ladies ... who live on their manors ought to manage their households and estates"'. For coverture, see, most recently, Beattie, 'Married Women, Contracts and Coverture'; Butler, 'Discourse on the Nature of Coverture'; and Phipps, 'Coverture and the Marital Partnership'.
9. For the composition of local courts and their relationship to the parliamentary franchise, see Cam, *Law-Finders and Law-Makers*; Maddicott, 'County Community'; and Maddicott, 'Parliament and the Constituencies'.
10. SC 8/9/421. For the resulting action see *CCR, 1302–7*, 305–6. See also another iteration of the point by the same petitioner in SC 8/328/E890.
11. C 65/86, m. 3, printed in *RP*, IV, 270, and in *PROME*, X, 222. For Margaret Marshal, see Archer, 'Estates and Finances of Margaret of Brotherton'.
12. See, for example, Edwards, *Second Century*. For the ways in which parliament dealt with 'common' and 'private' petitions, see the extensive literature summarised in Dodd, *Justice and Grace*; and Ormrod, Killick and Bradford, eds, *Early Common Petitions*.

13. Pronay and Taylor, eds, *Parliamentary Texts*, 88. There remains a debate as to the dating of the *Modus*, with some scholars still preferring the idea of composition in the late fourteenth century: see Pronay and Taylor, eds, *Parliamentary Texts*, 22–31; and Kerby-Fulton and Justice, 'Reformist Intellectual Culture'.
14. Musson, *Medieval Law in Context*, 207.
15. Ormrod, Killick and Bradford, eds, *Early Common Petitions*, 209–12. For a further example, see the naming of three individuals (including one female) set to be advantaged by the statute *De natis ultra mare* of 1351: *SR*, I, 310.
16. Myers, 'Parliamentary Petitions'; Myers, 'Observations'; and Dodd, *Justice and Grace*, 156–96.
17. Dodd, *Justice and Grace*, 211–15; and Payling, 'Women and Parliament'. Paul Brand has made two major analyses of private petitions in the reign of Edward I, but approaches the subject in a gender-neutral manner: Brand, 'Petitions and Parliament'; and Brand, 'Understanding Early Petitions'.
18. SC 8/1/1-SC8/156/7768, and SC 8/314/E107-SC 8/316/E248. The second sub-set listed here comprises an original file of petitions submitted in Parliament in 1302. For the series in general, see *Index of Ancient Petitions*, 2–11. We must be cautious about assuming that absolutely every petition in this sequence has a parliamentary provenance. See, for example, SC 8/243/12118, which records the submission by Isabel Abel of Tamworth of a total of seven 'bills' to Edward III on 18 February, 26 March and 2 April [1342]. Six of these petitions survive, four of them in the 'Parliamentary Petitions' section of the Ancient Petitions: SC 8/88/4380; SC 8/88/4381; SC 8/88/4382; SC 8/88/4383; SC 8/247/12344; and SC 8/247/12345. The petitions are datable to 1342 on the basis that at least some of them were enclosed with C 81/283/14706, dated 7 May 1342. No Parliament was held in 1342, though a Great Council was summoned on 25 February for 8 April, and then prorogued on 15 March: Fryde, Greenway, Porter and Roy, eds, *Handbook of British Chronology*, 560. It should also be noted that the 'Parliamentary Petitions' section of the Ancient Petitions, like other sections in the series, includes some documents that are not petitions (usually supporting documentation provided at the time of submission or gathered by the Crown when the petition was under consideration) and occasionally has more than one petition in a sub-set of a single entry, the sub-set using an alphabetical sequence after the main petition number. All of this means that 7910 is a close estimate, rather than the actual number, of the petitions in the 'Parliamentary Petitions' section.
19. Dodd, 'Parliamentary Petitions?'. There is no particular reason to believe that the limited sequence primarily employed in the present analysis is not

typical of women's parliamentary petitions more generally, except perhaps in that the number of instances from Gascon petitioners appears unusually small. This may be because, at least on some occasions, Gascon petitions were determined as a separate group left for further consideration at the end of a parliamentary assembly and were then subject to separate filing: see *PROME*, IV, 276, 324. More generally for Gascon petitions, see Guilhem Pépin, 'Petitions from Gascony'; and Dodd, 'Petitions from the King's Dominions'. With regard to the English Crown's lordship of Ireland, Linda Mitchell has recently pointed out that women resident in England with landed property in Ireland actively used petitions to the king in the English Parliament as a means of advancing their causes in Ireland: Mitchell, 'Land(ladies) from a Distance', 240.

20. For the likelihood that women were more numerous than men at least in urban areas during the late Middle Ages, see Goldberg, 'Urban Identity'.
21. The question of women's agency and how it can be deconstructed from legal records is developed further below, 129–132. See the recent overview of the debate by Stretton, 'Women'.
22. For the rest of this paragraph, see Dodd, *Justice and Grace*; Dodd, 'Writing Wrongs'; Dodd and Petit-Renaud, 'Grace and Favour'; and Killick, 'Treason, Felony and Lollardy'.
23. For the growth of the jurisdiction of the Chancery, see Tucker, 'Early History of the Court of Chancery'; Haskett, 'Conscience, Justice and Authority'; Klinck, *Conscience, Equity and the Court of Chancery*; and Makowski, '*Deus est procurator fatuorum*'.
24. Beattie, *Medieval Single Women*, 24–31, 124–43.
25. See the case of Princess Isabella, daughter of Edward III, in 1378 (56); and that of Alice Perrers, as referred to by her second husband, William Windsor, in the same Parliament (57).
26. Among a large literature, see Barron and Sutton, eds, *Medieval London Widows*; Mate, *Daughters, Wives and Widows*; Friedrichs, 'The Remarriage of Elite Widows in the Later Middle Ages', *Florilegium* 23 (2006): 69–83; Loengard, '"Which may be said to be her own"'; Archer, 'War Widows'; and Mitchell, 'Joan de Valence'. The *Index of Ancient Petitions* is deceptive on the marital status of women, in many cases rendering 'widow of' as 'wife of'. In such cases I have checked the originals in order to establish to which category the relevant petition really belongs. In a few cases, in fact, it emerges that a woman might describe herself as 'wife of' a named man, whereas the substance of the petition makes it clear that the husband was, indeed, dead: see, for example, SC 8/34/1677; SC 8/69/3432; and SC 8/114/5700.

27. See, for example, Butler, 'Law as a Weapon'; Makowski, '*Deus est procurator fatuorum*'; Beattie, '"Your Oratrice"'; and Beattie, 'Married Women, Contracts and Coverture'.
28. Haskett, 'Medieval English Court of Chancery'.
29. Hawkes, '"[S]he will … protect and defend her rights boldly by law and reason …"', 153.
30. Beattie, 'Piece of the Puzzle'.
31. Dodd, *Justice and Grace*, 52–60, 164–9, 232–41.
32. For the volume and significance of private petitions submitted to Parliament after the mid-fourteenth century, see Dodd, 'Hidden Presence'; and Dodd, *Justice and Grace*, 116–24, 211–15. For women seeking direct access to the king's person via petitions, see Lacey, 'Petitioners for Royal Pardon', 59–60.
33. Benz St John, *Three Medieval Queens*, 9, drawing especially on Maurer, *Margaret of Anjou*, 5. See also, in general, Capp, 'Separate Domains?'; Coss, *The Lady in Medieval England*; Wheeler and Parsons, eds, *Eleanor of Aquitaine*; and Laynesmith, *Last Medieval Queens*. For a useful study of widows and the law set within theoretical approaches to power and status, see Mitchell, 'The Lady is a Lord'.
34. Goldberg, 'Fiction in the Archives'; Collette, *Performing Polity*; Miriam Müller, 'Peasant Women, Agency and Status'; Goldberg, 'Echoes, Whispers, Ventriloquisms'; and Kane, 'Women, Memory and Agency'.
35. Kaeuper, *War, Justice, and Public Order*, 134–83, 244, 264.
36. Crawford, *Letters of Medieval Women*; Watt, ed., *The Paston Women*; Richardson, '"A masterful woman"'; Daybell, *Women Letter-Writers*; Daybell, 'Letters'; and Daybell and Gordon, eds, *Women and Epistolary*.
37. See, for example, among an extensive literature, Goldberg, 'The Public and the Private'.
38. McNamara and Wemple, 'Medieval Women'.
39. Erler and Kowaleski, eds, *Women and Power in the Middle Ages*; and Erler and Kowaleski, eds, *Gendering the Master Narrative*.
40. Erler and Kowaleski, 'Introduction' (quote at 2).
41. Carpenter and MacLean, eds, *Power of the Weak*.
42. Bennett, *History Matters* (quotes at 2, 3). For a more recent contribution to theoretical gender studies of the Middle Ages, see Skinner, *Studying Gender*.
43. Tanner, ed., *Medieval Elite Women*.

References

Unpublished Primary Sources

Kew, The National Archives of the United Kingdom
C 65 Chancery: Parliament Rolls.
C 81 Chancery: Warrants for the Great Seal, Series I.
SC 8 Special Collections: Ancient Petitions.

Published Primary Sources

Bradford, Phil, and Alison K. McHardy, eds, *Proctors for Parliament: Clergy, Community and Politics, c. 1248–1539*, 2 vols, Canterbury and York Society 107–8 (Woodbridge, 2017–2018).

Brand, Paul, Seymour Phillips, W. Mark Ormrod, Geoffrey Martin, Chris Given Wilson, Anne Curry and Rosemary Horrox, eds, *The Parliament Rolls of Medieval England*, 16 vols (Woodbridge: Boydell, 2005).

Calendar of the Close Rolls Preserved in the Public Record Office, Henry III-Henry VII, 61 vols (London: Her/His Majesty's Stationery Office, 1892–1963).

Ormrod, W. Mark, Helen Killick and Phil Bradford, eds, *Early Common Petitions in the English Parliament, c. 1290–c. 1420*, Camden Society 5th ser. 52 (Cambridge, 2017).

Pronay, Nicholas and John Taylor, eds, *Parliamentary Texts of the Later Middle Ages* (Oxford: Oxford University Press, 1980).

Raithby, John, ed., *The Statutes of the Realm*, 11 vols (London: Record Commission, 1810–1828).

Strachey, J., ed., *Rotuli Parliamentorum*, 6 vols (London: Record Commission, 1767–1777).

Watt, Diane, ed., *The Paston Women: Selected Letters* (Cambridge: D. S. Brewer, 2004).

Published Secondary Sources

Archer, Rowena E., 'The Estates and Finances of Margaret of Brotherton, *c.* 1320–1399', *Historical Research* 60 (1987): 264–80.

Archer, Rowena E., '"How ladies … who live on their manors ought to manage their households and estates": Women as Landholders and Administrators in the Later Middle Ages', in *Women in Medieval English Society, c. 1200–c. 1500*, ed. P. J. P. Goldberg (Stroud: Sutton, 1997), 149–81.

Archer, Rowena E., 'War Widows', in *The Battle of Agincourt*, ed. Anne Curry and Malcolm Mercer (London: Royal Armouries, 2015), 216–25.

Barron, Caroline M. and Anne F. Sutton, eds, *Medieval London Widows, 1300–1500* (London: A&C Black, 1994).

Beattie, Cordelia, 'Married Women, Contracts and Coverture in Late Medieval England', in *Married Women and the Law in Premodern Northwest Europe*, ed. Cordelia Beattie and Matthew F. Stevens (Woodbridge: Boydell, 2013), 133–54.

Beattie, Cordelia, *Medieval Single Women: The Politics of Social Classification in Late Medieval England* (Oxford: Oxford University Press, 2007).

Beattie, Cordelia, 'A Piece of the Puzzle: Women and the Law as Viewed from the Late Medieval Court of Chancery', *Journal of British Studies* 58 (2019): 751–67.

Beattie, Cordelia, '"Your Oratrice": Women's Petitions to the Late Medieval Court of Chancery', in *Women, Agency and the Law, 1300–1700*, ed. Bronach Kane and Fiona Williamson, The Body, Gender and Culture 15 (London: Taylor & Francis, 2013), 17–29.

Bennett, Judith M., *History Matters: Patriarchy and the Challenge of Feminism* (Manchester: Manchester University Press, 2006).

Benz St John, Lisa, *Three Medieval Queens: Queenship and the Crown in Fourteenth-Century England* (New York: Palgrave, 2012).

Brand, Paul, 'Petitions and Parliament in the Reign of Edward I', *Parliamentary History* 23 (2004): 14–38.

Brand, Paul, 'Understanding Early Petitions: An Analysis of the Content of Petitions to Parliament in the Reign of Edward I', in *Medieval Petitions: Grace and Grievance*, ed. W. Mark Ormrod, Gwilym Dodd and Anthony Musson (York: York Medieval Press, 2009), 99–119.

Butler, Sara M., 'Discourse on the Nature of Coverture in the Later Medieval Courtroom', in *Married Women and the Law: Coverture in England and the Common Law World*, ed. Tim Stretton and Krista J. Kesselring (Montreal: McGill-Queen's University Press, 2013), 24–44.

Butler, Sara M., 'The Law as a Weapon in Marital Disputes: Evidence from the Late Medieval Court of Chancery, 1424–1529', *Journal of British Studies* 43 (2004): 291–316.

Cam, Helen M., *Law-Finders and Law-Makers in Medieval England: Collected Studies in Legal and Constitutional History* (London: Merlin, 1962).

Capp, B. S., 'Separate Domains? Women and Authority in Early Modern England', in *The Experience of Authority in Early Modern England*, ed. Paul Griffiths, Adam Fox and Steve Hindle (Basingstoke: Macmillan, 1996), 117–45.

Carpenter, Jennifer and Sally-Beth MacLean, eds, *Power of the Weak: Studies on Medieval Women* (Champaign, Illinois: University of Illinois Press, 1995).

Collette, Carolyn P., *Performing Polity: Women and Agency in the Anglo-French Tradition, 1385–1620* (Turnhout: Brepols, 2006).

Cooper, J. P. D. and Richard A. Gaunt, 'Architecture and Politics in the Palace of Westminster, 1399 to the Present', *Parliamentary History* 38 (2019): 1–16.

Coss, Peter, *The Lady in Medieval England* (Stroud: Sutton, 1998).

Crawford, Anne, *Letters of Medieval Women* (Stroud: Sutton, 2002).
Daybell, James, 'Letters', in Laura Lunger Knoppers, ed., *The Cambridge Companion to Early Modern Women's Writing* (Cambridge: Cambridge University Press, 2009), 181–93.
Daybell, James, *Women Letter-Writers in Tudor England* (Oxford: Oxford University Press, 2006).
Daybell, James and Andrew Gordon, eds, *Women and Epistolary Agency in Early Modern Culture, 1450–1690* (London: Routledge, 2016).
Dodd, Gwilym, 'The Hidden Presence: Parliament and the Private Petition in the Fourteenth Century', in *Expectations of the Law in the Middle Ages*, ed. Anthony Musson (Woodbridge: Boydell, 2001), 135–49.
Dodd, Gwilym, *Justice and Grace: Private Petitioning and the English Parliament in the Late Middle Ages* (Oxford: Oxford University Press, 2007).
Dodd, Gwilym, 'Parliamentary Petitions? The Origins and Provenance of the "Ancient Petitions" (SC 8) in the National Archives', in *Medieval Petitions: Grace and Grievance*, ed. W. Mark Ormrod, Gwilym Dodd and Anthony Musson (York: York Medieval Press, 2009), 12–46.
Dodd, Gwilym, 'Petitions from the King's Dominions: Wales, Ireland and Gascony, *c.* 1290–1410', in *The Plantagenet Empire, 1259–1453*, ed. Peter Crooks, David Green and W. Mark Ormrod (Donington: Shaun Tyas, 2016), 187–215.
Dodd, Gwilym, 'Writing Wrongs: The Drafting of Supplications to the Crown in Later Fourteenth-Century England', *Medium Aevum* 80 (2011): 217–46.
Dodd, Gwilym and Sophie Petit-Renaud, 'Grace and Favour: The Petition and its Mechanisms', in *Government and Political Life in England and France, c. 1300–c. 1500*, ed. Christopher Fletcher, Jean-Philippe Genet and John Watts (Cambridge: Cambridge University Press, 2015), 240–78.
Erler, Mary C. and Maryanne Kowaleski, eds, *Gendering the Master Narrative: Women and Power in the Middle Ages.* (Ithaca, NY: Cornell University Press, 2003).
Erler, Mary C. and Maryanne Kowaleski, 'Introduction. A New Economy of Power Relations: Female Agency in the Middle Ages', in Mary C. Erler and Maryanne Kowaleski, eds, *Gendering the Master Narrative: Women and Power in the Middle Ages* (Ithaca, NY: Cornell University Press, 2003), 1–16.
Erler, Mary C. and Maryanne Kowaleski, eds, *Women and Power in the Middle Ages* (London: University of Georgia Press, 1988).
Friedrichs, Rhoda L., 'The Remarriage of Elite Widows in the Later Middle Ages', *Florilegium* 23 (2006): 69–83.
Fryde, E. B., D. E. Greenway, S. Porter and I. Roy, eds, *Handbook of British Chronology* (Cambridge: Cambridge University Press, 1986).
Fryde, E. B. and Edward Miller, eds, *Historical Studies of the English Parliament*, 2 vols (Cambridge: Cambridge University Press, 1970).

Goldberg, P. J. P., 'Echoes, Whispers, Ventriloquisms: On Recovering Women's Voices from the Court of York in the Later Middle Ages', in *Women, Agency and the Law, 1300–1700*, ed. Bronach Kane and Fiona Williamson, The Body, Gender and Culture 15 (London: Taylor & Francis, 2013), 31–41.

Goldberg, P. J. P., 'Fiction in the Archives: The York Cause Papers as a Source for Later Medieval Social History', *Continuity and Change* 12 (1997): 425–45.

Goldberg, P. J. P., 'The Public and the Private: Women in the Pre-Plague Economy', in *Thirteenth Century England III*, ed. Peter R. Coss and S. D. Lloyd (Woodbridge: Boydell, 1991), 75–89.

Goldberg, P. J. P., 'Urban Identity and the Poll Taxes of 1377, 1379 and 1381', *Economic History Review* 2nd ser. 43 (1990): 194–216.

Harriss, G. L., *King, Parliament and Public Finance in Medieval England to 1369* (Oxford: Oxford University Press, 1975).

Haskett, Timothy S., 'Conscience, Justice and Authority in the Late-Medieval English Court of Chancery', in *Expectations of the Law in the Middle Ages*, ed. Anthony Musson (Woodbridge: Boydell, 2001), 151–63.

Haskett, Timothy S., 'The Medieval English Court of Chancery', *Law and History Review* 14 (1996): 245–313.

Hawkes, Emma, '"[S]he will … protect and defend her rights boldly by law and reason …": Women's Knowledge of Common Law and Equity Courts in Late-Medieval England', in *Medieval Women and the Law*, ed. Noël James Menuge (Woodbridge: Boydell, 2000), 145–61.

Index of Ancient Petitions, Public Record Office Lists and Indexes 1, rev. edn (New York: Kraus, 1966).

Kaeuper, Richard W., *War, Justice, and Public Order: England and France in the Later Middle Ages* (Oxford: Oxford University Press, 1988).

Kane, Bronach, 'Women, Memory and Agency in the Medieval English Church Courts', in Bronach Kane and Fiona Williamson, eds, *Women, Agency and the Law, 1300–1700*, The Body, Gender and Culture 15 (London: Taylor & Francis, 2013), 43–62.

Kerby-Fulton, Kathryn and Steven Justice, 'Reformist Intellectual Culture in the English and Irish Civil Service: The *Modus tenendi parliamentum* and its Literary Relations', *Traditio* 53 (1998): 149–202.

Killick, Helen, 'Treason, Felony and Lollardy: A Common Petition in the Hand of Richard Osbarn, Clerk of the Chamber of the Guildhall, 1400–*c.* 1437', *Historical Research* 89 (2016): 227–45.

Klinck, Dennis R., *Conscience, Equity and the Court of Chancery in Early Modern England* (Farnham: Ashgate, 2010).

Lacey, Helen, 'Petitioners for Royal Pardon in Fourteenth-Century England', in *Petitions and Strategies of Persuasion in the Middle Ages: The English Crown and the Church, c. 1200–c. 1500*, ed. Thomas W. Smith and Helen Killick (York: York Medieval Press, 2018), 40–63.

Laynesmith, Joanna, *The Last Medieval Queens: English Queenship, 1445–1503* (Oxford: Oxford University Press, 2005).

Loengard, Janet Senderowitz, '"Which may be said to be her own": Widows and Goods in Late-Medieval England', in *Medieval Domesticity: Home, Housing and Household in Medieval England*, ed. Maryanne Kowaleski and P. J. P. Goldberg (Cambridge: Cambridge University Press, 2008), 162–76.

McNamara, Jo Ann and S. F. Wemple, 'Medieval Women: Their Gain and Loss of Power', *Barnard Alumnae* 63 (1974), 8–11.

Maddicott, J. R., 'The County Community and the Making of Public Opinion in Fourteenth-Century England', *Transactions of the Royal Historical Society* 5th ser. 28 (1978): 27–43.

Maddicott, J. R., *The Origins of the English Parliament, 924–1327* (Oxford: Oxford University Press, 2010).

Maddicott, J. R., 'Parliament and the Constituencies, 1272–1377', in *The English Parliament in the Middle Ages*, ed. R. G. Davies and J. H. Denton (Manchester: Manchester University Press, 1981), 61–87.

Makowski, Elizabeth M., '*Deus est procurator fatuorum*: Cloistered Nuns and Equitable Decision-Making in the Court of Chancery', in *Law as Profession and Practice in Medieval.*

CHAPTER 2

Queens and Noblewomen in Parliament

Abstract In spite of the history of the medieval Parliament being written solely as a history of men, there is a small amount of evidence to demonstrate the active and passive influence of queens and noblewomen in parliamentary business. Queens' association with Parliament came partly through their performance of intercession on behalf of nobles and others disgraced by the Crown and in danger of capital punishment; there are a number of instances of such activity in the fourteenth century. Oddly, queens acting in effect as regents, as in the case of Margaret of Anjou in the fifteenth century, were generally denied any formal seat in Parliament, though it is quite likely that Margaret was present at some of the Parliaments later in her husband's reign. Noblewomen were assiduous petitioners in Parliament, not least when their husbands lost their lives and lands and the surviving members of the family looked to the king for acts of generosity. A few noblewomen—notably Blanche, Lady Wake, under Edward III—deployed considerable rhetorical skills in their written petitions as a means of catching the eye of the king and securing their own advantage.

Keywords Gender • Dower • Noblewomen • Parliament • Petitions • Queens • Women

W. M. Ormrod, *Women and Parliament in Later Medieval England*, The New Middle Ages,
https://doi.org/10.1007/978-3-030-45220-9_2

Introduction

A useful starting-point for an analysis of the role of women in Parliament is provided by the functions on the one hand of queens, and on the other of the wives (or sometimes mothers, grandmothers or other female relatives) of the laymen who received personal summonses to attend Parliament in their own right as members of the Lords. The only part of the medieval Westminster Palace where those who were not summoned as Lords or returned as members of the Commons might gain access to proceedings was in the Great Hall, which was sometimes used as the venue for the ceremonial opening speeches and concluding feasts.[1] There is no record in the parliament rolls or chronicles that queens or peeresses attended these occasions. If the king was absent, either because he was abroad on campaign or because he was indisposed, then his place in Parliament was always taken by his (male) heir or other close male relative, whether they were of age or not.[2] This stands in contrast to the role that queens sometimes played in other political institutions. Philippa of Hainault, for example, represented her husband Edward III at a meeting of the royal Council held at Northampton in 1336, when the king was in Scotland; and she seems also to have made a personal appearance at a meeting of the Convocation of the clergy of the province of Canterbury in 1360, when Edward was in France, in order to plead the king's case for a grant of clerical taxation.[3] It is somewhat ironic, then, that one of the large rooms in the Privy Palace at Westminster that was used for the business of Parliament was known as the Queen's Chamber. This room became the regular place of meeting for the king and the Lords in the fifteenth century, and for the occasions when the Lords 'intercommuned' with deputations from the Commons—who by this stage, in turn, were generally meeting in the chapter house or refectory of Westminster Abbey.[4] Women of any status seem, therefore, to have been distinctly absent from the various levels of access that men, as a result of rank or office, had to the workings of the late medieval English Parliament.

Queens and Parliament

The 'male-only' character of Parliament can be taken as an important example of a more general phenomenon observed by historians of medieval queenship, whereby a court-centred political system in the high Middle Ages gave way, after the thirteenth century, to the institutionalised and solely masculine performance of government through Great Councils, Parliaments and offices of state. Whereas queens were significant players in the former system, they were thoroughly marginalised, if not formally banned, from the latter.[5] A series of revisionist studies published since the 1990s has, however, challenged this model by demonstrating the significant informal influence that queens continued to enjoy in the system of government during the thirteenth to fifteenth century through their presence in the ceremonial court and their *ex officio* interventions (for themselves and for others) in the royal household, the Council, the Chancery, the Privy Seal Office and the Exchequer.[6] If such a pattern of activity is also evident in Parliament, then the queen might, after all, be recognised to have had at least an informally recognised role to play in the business of high politics.

One relatively predictable aspect of such a presence relates to the queen's role as intercessor for royal mercy. A number of scholars, especially Paul Strohm, Lois Huneycutt and John Carmi Parsons, have shown how the king's wife—or, in her absence, his mother—was regarded as the personification of mercy, the quality of judgment that allowed the monarch to remit or ameliorate the full force of the law as it fell on those found guilty of high crimes.[7] Some at least of the set pieces in which the queen pleaded grace and pardon for offenders took place in Parliament. In the assembly that followed the Peasants' Revolt of 1381, for example, much was made of the recent arrival in the country of Anne of Bohemia and of her impending marriage to the young Richard II. In providing a rationalisation of the policy of reconciliation that the government wished to take towards those who had rebelled earlier in the year, the clerk of Parliament noted that the king's pardons were made 'out of reverence for God and his sweet mother St Mary, and at the special request of the noble lady, the Lady Anne, ... soon, if it please God, to be queen of England'.[8] The formal record does not go as far as saying that Anne was actually present in Parliament for such an announcement, and the fact that she was still being prepared for her wedding and coronation may suggest that she was purposely kept from the public gaze at this moment. Similarly, in 1384 the well-informed Westminster Chronicle claimed that Anne prayed mercy (unsuccessfully) for the Londoner John Northampton during a Great Council of Lords held at Reading, but does not specify the queen's actual attendance with the king at the performance of this ritual.[9] In the Merciless Parliament of 1388 Anne again made desperate representations, in vain, for the release from the death penalty of her husband's former tutor, Sir

Simon Burley. In this instance, we know that the intercession was directed specifically at the duke of Gloucester, one of the Lords Appellant, but the source is again unclear on how Anne interacted with the wider membership of Parliament on this occasion.[10]

Anne of Bohemia's successor, the infant Isabella of France, who was married to Richard II just before her seventh birthday in 1396 and was crowned the following year, seems to have been invested with sufficient authority for the Kirkstall chonicler to believe that she acted as intercessor for the earl of Warwick in the so-called Revenge Parliament of 1397 and successfully secured the commutation of his death sentence into perpetual exile on the Isle of Man.[11] While questions have again to be asked about whether the child-bride was actually brought into the Parliament chamber for this act of high political drama, it is clear from the cases of Richard II's wives that the queen's intercessory powers were explicitly brought into play in order to justify what might otherwise have been considered as 'unmanly' meekness on the part of the king.[12] More broadly, Archbishop Thomas Arundel stated in the first Parliament of Henry IV that England had 'for a long time been led, ruled and governed by children and by the advice of widows'.[13] While the reference to children was taken up and developed by Arundel into a sharp contrast between the childish Richard II and the mature Henry Bolingbroke, the point about widows was not elaborated. It may in part at least be a reference to the fact that Richard's mother, Joan of Kent, Princess of Wales (d. 1385) had fulfilled the role of intercessor with the king between her own widowhood in 1376 and Richard's marriage to Anne of Bohemia in 1382.[14]

It is interesting to compare the successful acts of intercession by Richard II's queens with the role of royal and noble women during the civil war at the end of Henry VI's reign and the beginning of Edward IV's. In the bill of attainder brought in the Coventry Parliament of 1459, Henry VI's government accused Richard, duke of York and his associates of 'diabolical inhumanity' (*diabolique unkyndnesse*) in the pursuit of their ambitions against the king.[15] According to one of the London chronicles, some of York's lesser supporters were allowed to come into the Parliament chamber 'in hair shirts and [with] halters in their hands' (*in hyr schyrtes and halters in hyr hondys*) in order to beg forgiveness. The king accepted their public act of contrition and duly released them from further punishment. In addition, the same chronicle claims that Cecily (née Neville), duchess of York took the role of female intercessor in pleading for her husband, the rebellious Richard Plantagenet. The relevant passage does not actually say that this mini-drama took place in Parliament, but it explicitly places it at and during the time of the assembly at Coventry.[16] The general refusal of the Lancastrian regime to bend to the clemency usually won through such performative devices was doubly significant given that the monarchy was effectively headed by Henry VI's queen, Margaret of Anjou; the depictions of Margaret in contemporary sources as a virago played very consciously on her own refusal to be constrained by traditional models of queenly duty and to assume the masculine responsibilities of military and political leadership.[17] While it is possible that Margaret's elevated status allowed her to do what other queens failed to achieve, and sit in her own right in Parliament, there is no mention of her in the passage relating to the duchess of York. This may signal the fact that Margaret consciously excused herself from this particular sitting in order to allow Cecily to assert, in uncompromised fashion, her own powers of supplication.

In spite of their normal physical absence from the various buildings at Westminster (and occasionally elsewhere) in which Parliament and its constituent elements met, queens, represented by members of their councils, regarded Parliament as an appropriate place in which to do their own public business. The negotiation and approval of the queen's dower was an important case in point. In the fourteenth century, queens' councillors saw no need to seek parliamentary legitimacy for the settlement of lands and rights assigned to the king's wife, and which provided her with an independent source of income not just while she was the consort but also in her widowhood.[18] The sensitivity with which Edward III and Richard II asserted their control over their own Chamber estate and household finances meant that their queens, too, were protected from public scrutiny of their income and expenditure.[19] This changed after 1399, when, under severe pressure resulting from the widespread dispersal of lands to support the new regime of Henry IV, both the Crown and successive queens looked to Parliament to support the re-endowment of the king's wife.[20] Following Henry's marriage to Joan of Navarre in 1403, the Commons in the Parliament of January 1404 forwarded a petition from the queen requesting the fulfilment of the letters patent granted to her upon her marriage, and which endowed upon her an estate worth 10,000 marks (£6667) a year.[21] In 1404, 1406, 1409 and 1410 the Commons followed up with further petitions for the delivery of the necessary lands.[22] In fact, Joan of Navarre's dower remained a point of disagreement up to and beyond Henry IV's death. Following Henry V's cynical effort in 1419 to condemn Joan as a witch and use her lands to contribute to his war effort, her ministers continued after her rehabilitation in 1422 to petition in Parliament for adequate resources to support her in widowhood.[23] The way in which Joan's petitions were adopted and forwarded by the Commons suggests the desire of her advisers to have the matter seen to be of public importance and/or the will of the Commons to see the queen properly resourced up to—but not beyond—a given point.

Joan of Navarre's repeated persistence as petitioner via the Commons set a precedent for the next queen, Katherine of Valois who, as a dowager, petitioned in 1422, 1423 and 1433 for the full delivery of her entitlement to a separate landed income.[24] The dower arrangements for Margaret of Anjou were submitted to Parliament in the form of a petition from the queen in 1447, and referred there again in 1453 and 1459, though on these latter occasions in documentation provided directly by the Crown.[25] Katherine of Valois was also apparently subjected to a statutory instrument approved in the Parliament of October 1427 that prevented dowager queens from marrying without the express permission of the reigning monarch.[26] In these narrow senses at least, the fifteenth century saw the fulfilment of the statement in the early-fourteenth-century tract, the *Modus tenendi parliamentum* ('Method of Holding Parliament'), that the primary business of Parliament was 'war if there is a war, and other matters concerning the persons of the king, *queen*, and their children' (emphasis added).[27]

By the same token, Parliament was also a place in which private individuals and institutions petitioned about business undertaken by the queen but not, for various reasons, yet enacted. The abbot of Vale Royal (Cheshire) petitioned in Parliament about the failure of the estate of the deceased Eleanor of Castile to pay a sum of money that this queen had promised towards the endowment of the abbey.[28] Occasionally, women and men who had appealed to the queen for her intervention with the king to deliver acts of grace such as pardons petitioned in Parliament in order to follow up on actions unfulfilled or requiring further royal intervention.[29] Most interesting in this regard, however, are petitions addressed directly *to* the queen in the context of parliamentary sessions. These appear to be very largely restricted to the exceptional circumstances that arose during the deposition crisis of 1326–1327 and the genuine confusion that petitioners then had over the source of royal authority during the transition of power between Edward II and his son and successor, the teenaged Edward III. As Shelagh Sneddon has shown, a number of the petitions presented to the Parliament of January 1327 (summoned originally in the name of Edward II) were addressed to the king, queen and prince, in recognition of the informal role that Queen Isabella had in effecting the regime change.[30] There are, however, a handful of other petitions within the sequence of 'Parliamentary Petitions' that are addressed specifically and solely to queens: one to Margaret of France in *c.* 1306; one to Queen Isabella in 1322; and one to Queen Philippa in 1333.[31] Anthony Musson has also identified two petitions addressed by Joan of Navarre effectively forwarding requests for royal favour for named individuals; one of these at least was probably submitted to the king and Council within the context of Parliament.[32]

Noblewomen and Parliament

Noblewomen feature prominently among petitioners to Parliament across the later Middle Ages, and especially so in the fifteenth century when the general profile of parliamentary petitions became more skewed towards the upper ranks of society.[33] Most of the aristocratic women who petitioned in this period did so as widows seeking some resolution of matters relating to their landed interests. In this sense, the petitions of noblewomen exemplify two contrasting points: the relative abundance in the later Middle Ages of 'rich old ladies', dowagers who controlled large tracts of land and the significant seigniorial powers that went with them; and the vulnerability of such women, who often found it difficult to secure their full rights in the face of open competition and occasional hostility from their own kindred.[34] In terms of sheer persistence, the prize for petitioning goes to Margaret Marshall (d. 1399), daughter and heiress of Thomas of Brotherton, earl of Norfolk (d. 1338) and, after 1397, recognised as duchess of Norfolk. There exist no fewer than twenty-one petitions (several of them being duplicates of each other) submitted by Margaret in Parliament over the course of Richard II's reign, all calling for the fulfilment of Edward I's endowment of the earldom of Norfolk.[35] Another assiduous petitioner was Elizabeth (née Burgherssh, d. 1402), widow of Edward, Lord Despenser, who after her husband's death in 1375 petitioned multiple times, first to have the wardship of their son, Thomas (later created earl of Gloucester by Richard II), and then to secure and uphold his legal interests and her rights to dower during their respective minority and widowhood.[36] In a later generation, Anne, dowager countess of Stafford (née of Gloucester, d. 1438), petitioned in Parliament twice in the early years of Henry VI for the enactment of an agreement made between her and Henry V, as co-heirs of the estate of Humphrey de Bohun, earl of Hereford and Northampton (d. 1373).[37]

All of the petitions of noblewomen hitherto specified were submitted in their own right under the status of widow, and therefore as *femme sole*. There are a number of cases, however, where women of high birth and marriage petitioned independently during the lifetimes of their husbands. In these instances, the supplicants looked deliberately to the kind of discretion that could be exercised by the king's Council in Parliament, which was not restricted by the rules of the common law, and by the prospect of immediate access to the king himself, who could accept a case simply as a matter of his own will. Princess Isabella, the eldest daughter of Edward III, married Enguerrand de Coucy, a French nobleman who was made earl of Bedford in the English peerage. On Edward III's death, however, Coucy renounced his allegiance to the English Crown and returned to his homeland to fight for the Valois cause in the Hundred Years War.[38] In the first Parliament of Richard II's reign, Isabella petitioned both for a grant of revenues to compensate her since her husband's defection and for the return to her of the manor of Kendal (Westmorland), unfairly taken from her by Edward III's discredited mistress, Alice Perrers, on the basis of a spurious charter allegedly made by Coucy. In the latter instance, the petition explicitly referred to Isabella's *de facto* status as *femme sole* as a result of her husband's desertion of the country and of the effective end of their marriage. As a single woman, she remarked, she was properly deserving of the aid of the king and Council.[39]

The most interesting case of a noblewoman asserting *femme sole* status in Parliament while still being married is that of Blanche (d. 1380), daughter of Henry, earl of Lancaster (d. 1345) and wife of Thomas, Lord Wake of Liddel (d. 1349). In 1320, when she was only a teenager, Blanche submitted a petition in Parliament claiming her right to justice on the grounds that her parents were out of the country and her husband was on pilgrimage to Compostella; there had been an attack on one of Thomas' manors, and Blanche requested the issue of a commission of oyer and terminer to inquire into the matter. As un-contentious as the matter may seem, the king's Council in Parliament was punctilious and rejected the petition specifically on the grounds that, as a married woman, Blanche had no right to have an action in her own name.[40]

This outcome provides a nice contrast with Blanche's altogether more favourable treatment in Parliament during her widowhood. In 1355, the dowager Lady Wake submitted a petition to Parliament concerning a long-standing feud between her people and those of the bishop of Ely, Thomas de Lisle. Having recounted the bishop's scurrilous efforts to ensure that she was denied justice in the courts, in which Blanche appears, as was conventional in petitions, in the third person, the text then breaks away from convention and adopts the first person, a hallmark of the letter form, in order to make a direct and very personal appeal to the supplicant's cousin, the king:

> Wherefore I ask my lord the king that if he may not properly reach a decision at this time, that he will wholly take the dispute into his most gracious hand until he is of leisure to try it, and that it shall not be tried outside his presence. This, most honoured lord, it is wished might be done for the love of God, at the request of the said Blanche.[41]

The record of the case on the parliament roll records that the king granted Blanche's final request and declared with his own mouth, 'I take the dispute into my hand'.[42] As a result, Edward III proceeded with a highly controversial confiscation of the bishop's temporalities that created serious political reverberations both in England and at the papal curia.[43] We shall see in Chap. 9 how, albeit exceptionally, other women could also deploy the rhetoric of the letter form and attract interest to their cases by expressing themselves in the first person.[44]

In spite of the fact that Margaret Marshall was specifically denied the right to be counted as a member of the parliamentary peerage, then, the roles taken by queens, noblewomen and their councillors in Parliament suggest that the king's Council was generally prepared to give special priority to the concerns of such high-born ladies in the public debates upon the Commons' business and in special consideration of noblewomen's private petitions. The failure of an Anne of Bohemia or a Cecily of York to have their special intercessions heard and acted upon in Parliament makes it clear that royal and aristocratic ladies enjoyed no automatic right to have their own way in state trials; while the dismissal of Blanche Wake's 1320 petition makes it clear that the Council in Parliament was reluctant to ignore the common law principles restricting the ability of married women to petition in their own right. Yet Edward III's decision to take personal charge of Lady Wake's cause against the bishop of Ely in her widowhood exemplifies a much wider cultural notion that the king should act as a champion of widows, other vulnerable women, and their children.[45] We shall see in the next chapter how this played out regularly in relation to the complaints brought to Parliament by women of gentry and lesser status.

Notes

1. For the public aspect of Westminster Hall and access to it by women, see Cooper and Gaunt, 'Architecture and Politics', 8–9.
2. See the ceremonial admission of the infant Richard of Bordeaux (the future Richard II) as president of the last Parliament of his ailing grandfather, Edward III, in C 65/31, mm. 9–8, printed in *RP*, II, 361–3, and in *PROME*, V, 394–8.
3. 1336: E 101/387/19, discussed by Benz St John, *Three Medieval Queens*, 136. 1359: E 359/3, rot. 44.
4. Caddick, 'The Painted Chamber', 29. See also, more generally, Hawkyard, 'From Painted Chamber to St Stephen's Chapel'; and Harrison, 'Parliament, MPs and the Buildings of Westminster'.
5. The classic statement is Facinger, 'Study of Medieval Queenship'. See also the recent useful survey by Earenfight, 'Lifetime of Power'.
6. See, amongst others: Parsons, 'Ritual and Symbol'; Wheeler and Parsons, eds, *Eleanor of Aquitaine*; Howell, *Eleanor of Provence*; Parsons, *Eleanor of Castile*; Benz St John, *Three Medieval Queens*; Maurer, *Margaret of Anjou*; and Laynesmith, *Last Medieval Queens*.
7. Strohm, *Hochon's Arrow*, 95–119; Huneycutt, 'Intercession'; Parsons, 'The Queen's Intercession'; Parsons, 'Intercessionary Patronage'; Musson, 'Queenship, Lordship and Petitioning'; Seabourne, *Imprisoning Medieval Women*, 184–6; and Benz St John, *Three Medieval Queens*, 33–64. Laynesmith, *Last Medieval Queens*, 139 argues that intercession was a less important element of the function of queens by the later fifteenth century.
8. C 65/37, m. 11, printed in *RP*, III, 103, and in *PROME*, VI, 223: 'al reverence de Dieux, et de sa doulce mere Seinte Marie, et al especiale requeste de noblee dame, dame Anne … roigne d'Engleterre, si Dieux plest, proscheinement avenir'. See also, more generally, Geaman, 'Beyond Good Queen Anne'.
9. Hector and Harvey, eds, *Westminster Chronicle*, 91–5. For the Great Council, see *CCR, 1381–5*, 470.
10. Hector and Harvey, eds, *Westminster Chronicle*, 328–32. See also Richard II's reference to this event in 1397, according to the *Eulogium historiarum*: Given-Wilson, ed. and trans., *Chronicles of the Revolution*, 65.
11. Given-Wilson, ed. and trans., *Chronicles of the Revolution*, 96.
12. For the 'unmanliness' of Richard II, see Fletcher, *Richard II*, 1–24.

13. C 65/62, m. 21, printed in *RP*, III, 415, and in *PROME*, VIII, 9: '… avoit estee par longe temps mesnez, reulez and governez par enfauntz et conseil des vefves …'.
14. Ormrod, 'In Bed with Joan of Kent'. Note also Thomas Haxey's complaint in 1397 about the king's over-reliance on bishops and ladies (*dames*): C 65/56, m. 6, printed in *RP*, III, 339, and in *PROME*, VII, 314; and Fletcher, *Richard II*, 246–7.
15. C65/104, m. 1, printed in *RP*, V, 347, and in *PROME*, XII, 457.
16. Gairdner, ed., *Historical Collections*, 206–7; commentary in *PROME*, XII, 450–1; and Ormrod, 'Pardon, Parliament and Political Performance', 301–3.
17. Maurer, *Margaret of Anjou*, 208–11.
18. This is not to say that earlier queens did not use Parliament as a place in which to advance their rights. See petitions from Eleanor of Provence and Margaret of France, the mother and second wife of Edward I, concerning disputes of land and the right to take a tallage on the queen's estates: SC 8/2/69; SC 8/92/4583; and SC 8/126/6270. Margaret of France also petitioned in Parliament for the advancement of the estate of her two sons: SC 8/60/2973.
19. See, however, the suggestion that Edward I discussed the dower arrangements of Eleanor of Castile in the Parliament of October 1275: commentary in *PROME*, I, 28.
20. Wolffe, *Royal Demesne*, 56, 87, 95, 107, 108, 111, 137.
21. C 65/66, m. 10, printed in *RP*, III, 532–3, and in *PROME*, VIII, 250–1.
22. C 65/67, m. 4, printed in *RP*, III, 555, and in *PROME*, VIII, 307; C 65/68, m. 17, printed in *RP*, III, 577, and in *PROME*, VIII, 348; *CPR, 1408–13*, 85–7; SC 8/23/1116, enrolled on the parliament roll at C 65/71, m. 12, and printed from there in *RP*, III, 632–3, and in *PROME*, VIII, 477–8; and Given-Wilson, *Henry IV*, 313–14. See also SC 8/80/3963, which must have been submitted in one of the Parliaments immediately following Henry IV's marriage to Joan, as it requests that the custody of the lands of the earl of Stafford (d. 1403).
23. C 65/85, m. 25, printed in *RP*, IV, 247, and in *PROME*, X, 173–6; summary of documentation in *PROME*, X, 315; and Myers, *Crown, Household and Parliament*, 93–134.
24. C 65/84, mm. 7–4, printed in *RP*, IV, 183–9, and in *PROME*, X, 43–55; C 65/85, mm. 5–4, printed in *RP*, IV, 201–6, and in *PROME*, X, 87–95; and SC 8/119/5933 (A and B), summarised in *PROME*, XI, 154.
25. C 65/98, m. 4, printed in *RP*, V, 133–4, and in *PROME*, XII, 19–22; C 65/102, m. 7, printed in *RP*, V, 258–63, and in *PROME*, XII, 294–303; and C 65/104, m. 4, printed in *RP*, V, 352, and in *PROME*, XII, 467–8.

26. The discussions in *PROME*, X, 324–5, 365, provide full bibliographical references on the debate about this 'missing' statute.
27. Pronay and Taylor, eds, *Parliamentary Texts*, 75, 88: 'primo de guerra si guerra sit, et de aliis negotiis personas regis, regine et suorum liberorum tangetibus.'
28. SC 8/145/7247.
29. For example, William Herbert, prior of Ware reminded Richard II of a request made by the latter's late mother, Joan of Kent (who had fulfilled the role of queenly intercessor before Richard's marriage to Anne of Bohemia): SC 8/146/7262. For other petitions outside the run of 'Parliamentary Petitions' that remind the Crown of the interventions of queens, see, for example: SC 8/194/9661 (intervention of Isabella of France [d. 1358]); and SC 8/185/9240 (intervention of Katherine of France).
30. Sneddon, 'Words and Realities', 199–200. The petitions thus identified by Sneddon are SC 8/18/853; SC 8/46/2256; and SC 8/74/3669. For a further petition to the 'queen and [the] duke [of Aquitaine]' that may have been heard in the first Parliament of Edward III's reign, see SC 8/307/15309, printed in *RP*, II, 381, and noted in *PROME*, III, 463. For further discussion of the context, see Benz St John, *Three Medieval Queens*, 139–61.
31. Margaret: SC 8/39/1904; Musson, 'Queenship, Lordship and Petitioning', 160. Isabella: SC 8/55/2731, discussed by Musson, 'Queenship, Lordship and Petitioning', 161; and by Seabourne, *Imprisoning Medieval Women*, 185. Philippa: SC 8/307/15308, printed in *RP*, II, 72 and noted in *PROME*, III, 461.
32. Musson, 'Queenship, Lordship and Petitioning', 161, citing SC 8/158/7900 and SC 8/229/11420.
33. Dodd, *Justice and Grace*, 215–20.
34. For the 'rich old ladies' thesis and challenges to its typicality, see Archer, 'Rich Old Ladies'; and Friedrichs, 'Rich Old Ladies Made Poor'.
35. SC 8/19/933-948; SC 8/34/1663; SC 8/36/1788; SC 8/128/6355; SC 8/145/7219; and SC 8/166/8267. See also SC 8/129/6444; SC 8/130/6473. For the background, see Archer, 'Estates and Finances of Margaret of Brotherton', 264–80, where one enrolled petition out of this sequence is noted (271 n. 51). More generally on Margaret Marshall, see Mitchell, 'Maud Marshal and Margaret Marshal', 128–39.
36. SC 8/85/4205; SC 8/106/5275; SC 8/106/5288; SC 8/106/5293; SC 8/106/5295; SC 8/107/5316; and SC 8/158/7884.
37. SC 8/26/1268; and SC 8/26/1270.
38. Lutkin, 'Isabella de Coucy'.

39. SC 8/95/4710, leading to *CPR, 1377–81*, 174–5; and SC 8/41/2011, published by Bain, ed., 'Petition by the Lady Isabella'; and discussed by Ormrod, 'Trials of Alice Perrers', 384. For Isabella's petition to recover lands confiscated from her husband on his defection, see SC 8/95/4710.
40. SC 8/87/4346.
41. C 65/19, m. 1, printed in *RP*, II, 267, and in *PROME*, V, 128: 'Par quoi jeo requere a monsir le roi qe s'il ne puisse deliverer bonement a cest foitz, q'il voile prendre entierment la querele en sa tresgraciouse main tantqe il soit leisir de trier, et qe ele ne soit mie trie hors de sa presence. Ceo voillez, treshonure seignur, faire pur l'amur de Dieu, a la requeste la dite Blaunche.' In letters, the *ars dictaminis* required that the author identify him/herself in the third person at the beginning of the text, but then move to the first person for the substance of the text: see, for example, the *exempla* for letters from husbands to wives and vice versa, in Carlin and Crouch, eds, *Lost Letters of Medieval Life*, 235–41. For petitionary form, see Dodd, *Justice and Grace*, 280–90. For further discussion of letter forms in early petitions in Parliament, see below, 127–131.
42. C 65/19, m. 1, printed in *RP*, II, 267, and in *PROME*, V, 128: 'Jeo prenk la querele en ma main.'
43. For the full details of the dispute, see Aberth, *Criminal Churchmen*, 117–42.
44. See below, 129–132.
45. Rigby, *Wisdom and Chivalry*, 15–16.

References

Unpublished Primary Sources

Kew, The National Archives of the United Kingdom
C 65 Chancery: Parliament Rolls.
E 101 Exchequer: King's Remembrancer: Accounts Various.
E 359 Exchequer: Pipe Office: Account Rolls of Subsidies and Aids.
SC 8 Special Collections: Ancient Petitions.

Published Primary Sources

Bain, Joseph, ed., 'Petition by the Lady Isabella, Countess of Bedford … to the Council of Richard II …', *Archaeological Journal* 36 (1879): 174–6.
Brand, Paul, Seymour Phillips, W. Mark Ormrod, Geoffrey Martin, Chris Given Wilson, Anne Curry and Rosemary Horrox, eds, *The Parliament Rolls of Medieval England*, 16 vols (Woodbridge: Boydell, 2005).

Calendar of the Close Rolls Preserved in the Public Record Office, Henry III-Henry VII, 61 vols (London: Her/His Majesty's Stationery Office, 1892–1963).
Calendar of the Patent Rolls Preserved in the Public Record Office, Henry III–Henry VII, 54 vols (London: Her/His Majesty's Stationery Office, 1891–1916).
Carlin, Martha and David Crouch, eds, *Lost Letters of Medieval Life: English Society, 1200–1250* (Philadelphia: University of Pennsylvania Press, 2013).
Gairdner, James, ed., *The Historical Collections of a Citizen of London in the Fifteenth Century*, Camden Society new ser. 17 (London, 1876).
Given-Wilson, Chris, ed. and trans., *Chronicles of the Revolution, 1397–1400* (Manchester: Manchester University Press, 1993).
Hector, L. C. and Barbara F. Harvey, eds, *The Westminster Chronicle, 1381–1394* (Oxford: Clarendon Press, 1982).
Pronay, Nicholas and JohnTaylor, eds, *Parliamentary Texts of the Later Middle Ages* (Oxford: Oxford University Press, 1980).
Strachey, J., ed., *Rotuli Parliamentorum*, 6 vols (London: Record Commission, 1767–1777).

Published Secondary Sources

Aberth, John, *Criminal Churchmen in the Age of Edward III: The Case of Bishop Thomas de Lisle* (University Park, Pennsylvania: Pennsylvania State University Press, 1996).
Archer, Rowena E., 'The Estates and Finances of Margaret of Brotherton, *c.* 1320–1399', *Historical Research*60 (1987): 264–80.
Archer, Rowena E., 'Rich Old Ladies: The Problem of Medieval Dowagers', in *Property and Politics: Essays in Later Medieval History*, ed. A. J.Pollard (Gloucester: Sutton, 1984), 15–31.
Benz St John, Lisa, *Three Medieval Queens: Queenship and the Crown in Fourteenth-Century England* (New York: Palgrave, 2012).
Caddick, Jennifer, 'The Painted Chamber at Westminster and the Openings of Parliament, 1399–1484', *Parliamentary History* 38 (2019): 17–33.
Cooper, J. P. D. and Richard A.Gaunt, 'Architecture and Politics in the Palace of Westminster, 1399 to the Present', *Parliamentary History* 38 (2019): 1–16.
Dodd, Gwilym, *Justice and Grace: Private Petitioning and the English Parliament in the Late Middle Ages* (Oxford: Oxford University Press, 2007).
Earenfight, Theresa, 'A Lifetime of Power: Beyond Binaries of Gender', in *Medieval Elite Women and the Exercise of Power, 1100–1400: Moving Beyond the Exceptionalist Debate*, ed. Heather J. Tanner (Basingstoke: Palgrave Macmillan, 2019), 271–93.
Facinger, Marion, 'A Study of Medieval Queenship: Capetian France, 987–1328', *Nebraska Studies in Medieval and Renaissance History* 5 (1968): 1–48.

Fletcher, Christopher D., *Richard II: Manhood, Youth and Politics, 1377–99* (Oxford: Oxford University Press, 2008).

Friedrichs, Rhoda L., 'Rich Old Ladies Made Poor: The Vulnerability of Women's Property in Late Medieval England', *Medieval Prosopography* 21 (2000): 211–29.

Geaman, Kristen L., 'Beyond Good Queen Anne: Anne of Bohemia, Patronage, and Politics', in *Medieval Elite Women and the Exercise of Power, 1100–1400: Moving Beyond the Exceptionalist Debate*, ed. Heather J. Tanner (Basingstoke: Palgrave Macmillan, 2019), 67–89.

Given-Wilson, Chris, *Henry IV* (London: Yale University Press, 2016).

Harrison, David, 'Parliament, MPs and the Buildings of Westminster in the Middle Ages', in *Westminster II: The Art, Architecture and Archaeology of the Royal Palace*, ed. Warwick Rothwell and Tim Tatton-Brown (Leeds: Maney, 2015), 133–51.

Hawkyard, Alasdair, 'From Painted Chamber to St Stephen's Chapel: The Meeting Places of the House of Commons at Westminster until 1603', *Parliamentary History* 21 (2002): 62–84.

Huneycutt, Lois, 'Intercession and the High-Medieval Queen', in *Power of the Weak: Studies on Medieval Women*, ed. JenniferCarpenter and Sally-Beth MacLean (Champaign, Illinois: University of Illinois Press, 1995), 126–46.

Howell, Margaret, *Eleanor of Provence: Queenship in Thirteenth-Century England* (Oxford: Oxford University Press, 1998).

Laynesmith, Joanna, *The Last Medieval Queens: English Queenship, 1445–1503* (Oxford: Oxford University Press, 2005).

Lutkin, Jessica, 'Isabella de Coucy, Daughter of Edward III: The Exception who Proves the Rule', in *Fourteenth Century England VI*, ed. Chris Given-Wilson (Woodbridge: Boydell, 2010), 131–48.

Maurer, Helen, *Margaret of Anjou: Queenship and Power in Late Medieval England* (Woodbridge: Boydell, 2003).

Mitchell, Linda E., 'Maud Marshal and Margaret Marshal: Two Viragos Extraordinaire', in *The Ties That Bind: Essays in Medieval British History in Honor of Barbara Hanawalt*, ed. Linda E. Mitchell, Katherine L. French and Doulas L. Biggs (Frarnham: Ashgate, 2011), 121–42.

Musson, Anthony, 'Queenship, Lordship and Petitioning in Late Medieval England', in *Medieval Petitions: Grace and Grievance*, ed. W. Mark Ormrod, Gwilym Dodd and Anthony Musson (York: York Medieval Press, 2009), 156–72.

Myers, A. R., *Crown, Household and Parliament in Fifteenth-Century England* (London: Hambledon, 1985).

Ormrod, W. Mark, 'In Bed with Joan of Kent: The King's Mother and the Peasants' Revolt', in *Medieval Women: Texts and Contexts in Late Medieval Britain. Essays for Felicity Riddy*, ed. Jocelyn Wogan-Browne et al. (Turnhout: Brepols, 2000), 277–92.

Ormrod, W. Mark, 'Pardon, Parliament and Political Performance in Later Medieval England', in *Prowess, Piety, and Public Order in Medieval Society: Studies in Honor of Richard W. Kaeuper*, ed. Craig M. Nakashian and Daniel P. Franke (Leiden: Brill, 2017), 301–20.

Ormrod, W. Mark, 'The Trials of Alice Perrers', *Speculum* 83 (2008): 366–96.

Parsons, John Carmi, *Eleanor of Castile: Queen and Society in Thirteenth-Century England* (New York: Palgrave Macmillan, 1998).

Parsons, John Carmi, 'The Intercessionary Patronage of Queens Margaret and Isabella of France', in *Thirteenth Century England VI*, ed. Michael Prestwich, Richard H. Britnell and Robin Frame (Woodbridge: Boydell, 1997), 145–56.

Parsons, John Carmi, 'The Queen's Intercession in Thirteenth-Century England', in *Power of the Weak: Studies on Medieval Women*, ed. Jennifer Carpenter and Sally-Beth MacLean (Champaign, Illinois: University of Illinois Press, 1995), 147–77.

Parsons, John Carmi, 'Ritual and Symbol in the English Medieval Queenship to 1500', in *Women and Sovereignty*, ed. Louisa O. Fradenburg (Edinburgh: Edinburgh University Press, 1992), 60–77.

Rigby, Stephen H., *Wisdom and Chivalry: Chaucer's* Knight's Tale *and Medieval Political Theory* (Leiden: Brill, 2009).

Seabourne, Gwen, *Imprisoning Medieval Women: The Non-Judicial Confinement and Abduction of Women in England, c. 1170–1509* (Farnham: Ashgate, 2011).

Sneddon, Shelagh A., 'Words and Realities: The Language and Dating of Petitions, 1326–7', in *Medieval Petitions: Grace and Grievance*, ed. W. Mark Ormrod, Gwilym Dodd and Anthony Musson (York: York Medieval Press, 2009), 193–205.

Strohm, Paul, *Hochon's Arrow: The Social Imagination of Fourteenth-Century* Texts (Princeton: Princeton University Press, 1992).

Wheeler, Bonnie and John Carmi Parsons, eds, *Eleanor of Aquitaine: Lord and Lady* (Basingstoke: Macmillan, 2002).

Wolffe, B. P., *The Royal Demesne in English History: The Crown Estate in the Governance of the Realm from the Conquest to 1509* (London: Allen & Unwin, 1971).

CHAPTER 3

Women of the Gentry and Lesser Social Status

Abstract Petitions to the Crown in Parliament from women of gentry and lesser social status fall into a number of sub-categories. Petitions from women acting on their own behalf, as *femmes soles* or independent women (often, though not always, widows) cover a multiplicity of causes, but often present a gendered view by casting the source of the petitioner's troubles in terms of the greater power enjoyed by male protagonists. Discourses of poverty and helplessness are therefore a regular part of the rhetorical strategy deployed by female petitioners. Petitions from women as wives of named husbands generally arose where there was a dispute over land to which the wife, rather than the husband, had the formal claim. There were, however, a number of instances in which women could petition on their own, in the absence of their husbands: when the latter were held in gaol, or were prisoners of war, or were otherwise abroad on pilgrimage, etc. The chapter concludes with a detailed discussion of the petition of Margaret Basset against Sir Richard Stanhope, heard in the Leicester Parliament of 1414, when Margaret herself may have been present for proceedings.

Keywords Gender • Gentry • Marriage • Parliament • Peasants • Single-woman

W. M. Ormrod, *Women and Parliament in Later Medieval England*, The New Middle Ages,
https://doi.org/10.1007/978-3-030-45220-9_3

Introduction

The files of 'Parliamentary Petitions' within the longer sequence of the Ancient Petitions provide abundant evidence of the activities of women below the ranks of the peerage as supplicants in and to Parliament during the later Middle Ages. The vast majority of petitions identified in Table 1.1 as made in the joint names of husbands and wives or in the name of a woman defining herself as a daughter refer to disputes over the inheritance of land. As Simon Payling has shown from the inquisitions *post mortem* of tenants in chief of the Crown, the proportion of estates passing through the female line increased significantly during the period 1350–1450.[1] The growth in the number of heiresses placed a strain on the legal system as officials, male relatives and other third parties attempted to deprive women from asserting their rights of inheritance. In 1302, three of the daughters of Thomas le Raggedd—Joan, Emma and Agnes, all unmarried—claimed that a parcel of land bought by a fourth sister, Elizabeth, now a nun, ought not to be subject to the seizure of their deceased father's main estate by the royal escheator.[2] A clutch of petitions made jointly by Robert de Bilkemore and his wife, Anastasia, in the late 1330s, referred to rights that Anastasia had inherited both from her father, William de Harden, and from her first husband, Nicholas de Kyngeston; in one of these petitions, from 1334, the couple specifically complained that their case had been referred to Parliament but had then been adjourned without judgment from session to session, to their great cost and trouble.[3] It is important to recognise that married women were formally included alongside their husbands because they were direct stakeholders in the relevant cases. Early in the fourteenth century, for example, John Veys of Bristol and his wife Catherine, whose first husband had been Terri de la Brewer, a merchant of Bruges in Flanders, made several petitions in Parliament about the complications that had arisen in their attempts to recover debts owed to Terri and which were theirs to recover since Catherine Veys was evidently both the beneficiary and the executrix of de la Brewer's will.[4]

Femmes Soles as Petitioners in Parliament

For present purposes, it is the group of petitions from women effectively acting as *femmes soles* that provides the most interest among the wider body of women's supplications in Parliament. Within this group, there is a considerable range of social groups and experiences. In the late thirteenth century, one Alice de Wytteneye submitted a petition in Parliament citing the unnamed wife of William Trotyn of Chipping Norton (Oxfordshire), from whom she had bought a loaf of bread. When Alice had complained about the size of the loaf, the Trotyns had had her beaten and imprisoned, maltreating her sufficiently that she had lost her unborn child.[5] In 1318, Anneys de Aldenby petitioned Parliament about the way she was being terrorised by a group of named servants and associates of the earl of Lancaster. Anneys had had her tongue cut out and her eyes put out by her enemies, and hoped not only to secure a commission of oyer and terminer to decide the matter but also in the interim that the offenders, being powerful people, would be imprisoned.[6] Amice de Houwe of Ringmer (Sussex), petitioning in Parliament in 1341, not only complained about a number of more powerful people who had blocked her paths to justice but also itemised a range of livestock, down to the individual cow and horse, that had been taken unjustly from her over the previous fourteen years.[7] In similar vein, the Payer sisters, Margery and Edith, of Salisbury, requested assistance against their rival Juete Faircok in 1348; Faircok, they noted, was a wealthy woman and therefore dangerously likely to be able to buy herself out of trouble.[8] Finally in 1455, Joan Martyn of Canterbury, bedeswoman, requested exemption from the act of resumption being made in Parliament so that she could continue to draw her royal grant of 14d. a week, paid to her because, during one of the king's visits to Canterbury, his yeoman Nicholas ap Rhys had cut off her hand.[9] Although petitioning in Parliament became a comparative rarity for women of lower status in the fifteenth century, participation by women who held manorial tenancies in the countryside or occupied the lower or middling ranks of urban society was quite prevalent in the late thirteenth and fourteenth centuries, and remained at least a possibility thereafter.

As these examples also demonstrate, female petitioners in Parliament, and/or the men who wrote their petitions, used a range of discourses that played on the idea of the woman as defenceless in the face of male aggression, whether that be through physical threats or in legal proceedings. Katherine Engayne, petitioning at some point in the reign of Richard II, complained that the power of her (male) opponents made it impossible to sue them at common law, and appealed to the king because she was a widow, 'without the governance of a husband' (*sanz governail de baroun*).[10] When Constance Haliday of Pontefract petitioned for the recovery of debts from the estate of the rebellious earl of Lancaster in 1322, she emphasised her neediness not only by registering herself as a widow but by claiming that her fifteen children were starving for want of money.[11] Juliana de Faversham petitioned in Parliament in 1305 because, as she claimed, she was being unjustly pursued for fictional debts of her husband in the Irish Exchequer; as a result, she and her children had been forced to leave Ireland and pursue Edward I around Scotland, presumably during the English king's wide-ranging campaign there in 1303–1304. One of the clerks responsible for sorting private petitions in Parliament wrote rather enigmatically on the dorse of this petition, 'For a woman' (*Pro muliere*).[12] There is no reason to suppose that this was meant pejoratively: indeed, it may be that it was a marker of the perceived responsibility of the Crown to care for women who were not under the coverture of men.

In this respect, while pleas of poverty and weakness in the face of (usually male) verbal or physical aggression were certainly not exclusive to women's petitions, the emotional force, when combined with the idea of female defencelessness, was arguably greater for women than for men.[13] In the early 1320s, a collective petition from a group of the townspeople of Canterbury complaining of various wrongs was forwarded with a covering petition from Alice Devery, 'a poor woman' (*pouvre femme*) of the city, with the apparent aim that Alice's pressing grievances and plight would prompt attention to the more general cause and deliver the commission of oyer and terminer requested.[14]

Married Women as Petitioners in Parliament

There are a number of categories of parliamentary petitions from women acting in their own right where it can be shown that their husbands were still alive. The brisk put-down that Blanche Wake had suffered when she tried to petition during her husband's absence on pilgrimage in 1320 is a reminder of the real restrictions that the common law placed on the ability of married women to act on their husbands' behalf. In 1318, Beatrice Ryhull, the widow of Richard de Knotton, and their daughter Agnes asked for a remedy against Philip de Montgomery, who had stolen the family's livestock four years earlier and had imprisoned Richard in the Marshalsea prison, where he had died; because Philip was now a member of the king's household, Beatrice and Agnes hoped that Edward II might intervene in person. The stern reply went back to the only point of law in the petition and noted that there was no action available in the courts allowing a wife to sue for the goods of her husband taken during his lifetime.[15] Similarly, Alisot Uphatherle petitioned in 1330, requesting remedy for her husband,

Henry, after a series of assaults on him by Robert Prestbury, who (she noted, no doubt to catch the king's eye) had been in the army with which Queen Isabella had invaded England in 1326. The dry response, however, was that everything depended on whether Henry was actually still alive or not.[16]

There were, however, other instances where the Crown was prepared to accept the idea that women could supplicate on behalf of, and/or in the absence of, living husbands. Three specific circumstances may be mentioned here. The first is that of married women who were in the process of divorce in the church courts and were concerned about the consequences of the common law process whereby a husband was allowed to demand that his estranged wife cohabit with him until the final annulment.[17] The Crown was careful not to cross the boundary with the ecclesiastical jurisdiction on such matters.[18] But it could also indicate its sympathy for women's plight. In 1305, Mabel de Surdeval petitioned the king in Parliament about her appeal against her husband, Peter de Frothingham, and insisted that she wished to live separately pending the divorce settlement from the papal court. The Council's response was that Mabel should go to the Chancery and, having proved that she was indeed prosecuting her appeal, would be given a remedy appropriate to the case.[19]

Another instance of married women acting independently in petitions presented in Parliament is that of alien women who married Englishmen and then sought letters of denization from the Crown so that they could have equivalent legal status to English-born women—especially, it would seem, in connection with their rights to dower.[20] In anticipation of the flood of cross-Channel marriages that might result from Henry V's new status as heir to the throne of France, the Parliament of 1420 requested confirmation that dower be guaranteed to all foreign women married to English men.[21] Although the Crown responded positively, the absence of a new statute on this matter seems to have raised questions about the degree to which the agreement would be honoured, and in later years a number of high-status women, including the wives of Henry VI's uncles, Anne of Burgundy, Jacqueline of Hainault and Jacquetta of Luxembourg, were declared denizens in Parliament.[22] More generally, although it was common enough for the husband, or the husband and wife jointly, to petition for the denization of foreign-born wives, there are a number of extant cases where married women petitioned in Parliament, in their own right, for such status.[23] In these instances the suitors took direct advantage of the special access to the king's grace offered during a session of Parliament. It should be emphasised that neither women nor men born outside the English realm and dominions had to seek denization in order to make other petitions to Parliament—for Parliament, like the other prerogative courts, was open to petitioners from all foreign lands.[24] Among many examples that could be cited is that of Margaret Sarnesfield (d. *c.* 1444), who was probably one of the high-born Czech ladies who arrived in the entourage of Anne of Bohemia in 1381–1382; Douglas L. Biggs' account of Margaret's long campaign, after her English husband's death, for securing possession of the lands and rights accorded to her by Richard II, including a petition to the Parliament of 1431, provides an important instance of a woman who never found it necessary to take out denization in order to give her access to the prerogative courts of England.[25]

The third significant category of petitions from married women acting in their own right concerns those female petitioners whose husbands were indisposed by poor health, by absence from the country on military service or pilgrimage, or more commonly because they were being held as prisoners either within England or abroad. In the late 1280s, Maud, the wife of Ralph le Butller of Wem (Shropshire) complained that she could not pursue a case in the courts in which she and her husband were joint plaintiffs because Ralph was ill.[26] In spite of the refusal of Edward II's Council in 1320 to allow Blanche Wake to take proceedings on her own account while her husband was on pilgrimage, this is precisely what Edward III's government allowed to Maud, the wife of another royal cousin and close associate of the king, Edmund de Bohun, in 1331.[27] In 1426, Margaret Cornish of Uxbridge (Middlesex) successfully petitioned in her own right to obtain a pardon for her husband, Thomas, who was imprisoned following his trial for felony in the court of King's Bench.[28] And Joan Felton petitioned early in Richard II's reign on behalf of her husband, Sir Thomas, who was a prisoner of war in Aquitaine, asking that the Crown apply diplomatic pressure on the French for his release.[29]

The Petition of Margaret Basset

One petition from a woman of gentry status presents an unusually detailed record that allows us to see a female petitioner apparently following her complaint all the way into a meeting of Parliament. In 1414, when Henry V moved the court of King's Bench to Leicester to undertake a campaign against lawlessness in the Midlands, Parliament was also called to meet in the town.[30] On 30 April, a petition from one Margaret Basset of Nottinghamshire against the prominent knight of the same county, Richard Stanhope, was heard before the king and the Lords.[31] The account of the hearing on the dorse of Basset's petition makes it clear that Stanhope was present in person, presumably because he had been summoned on this or another of the crimes alleged against him at the same time.[32] There is no such categorical statement that Margaret Basset was also present. However, the account of the case does say that 'the said Margaret, on the contrary, alleged …' (*la dite Margarete al encontre allege*[…]), which is either a shorthand way of referring back to the petition written on the face of the document or a slightly opaque way of saying that Margaret had made the journey to Leicester and was actually in the meeting before the king and the Lords. We know that a special hall was constructed in Leicester, next to the Franciscan friary, for the specific purposes of this Parliament, and it is possible that a slightly more liberal attitude was taken towards admission to this building than was the case at Westminster.[33]

Margaret Basset's petition is also unusual in the sense that it sets out in much more detail than many other such written plaints her allegations against Stanhope, including exact dates for a series of violent encounters that had taken place, she said, in 1406–1407 (though in point of fact more likely in 1404–1405, when Stanhope had been sheriff of Nottinghamshire). The charges included confiscation of her lands, assaults on her person, theft of her goods, intimidation by Stanhope's officers, and the confounding of other legal cases in which she had been involved; as a consequence of these oppressions, Margaret claimed, she had been forced to flee from Nottinghamshire (perhaps to the environs of Leicester?) and dared not return home. Stanhope insisted on his innocence. But Margaret or her representatives persisted in her accusations, and the king and Lords therefore decided that the matter needed to be referred elsewhere, leaving the details to a general commission of oyer and terminer appointed to investigate criminality in Nottinghamshire and Derbyshire.[34] Meanwhile, 'because … the said Richard was one of the most powerful and contentious people in the county and the said Margaret was a poor and simple widow', they felt it appropriate to have Stanhope arrested and kept in prison at Kenilworth Castle until such time as the matter came to trial.[35] The written summary of the case concludes with the king himself telling Margaret—in what looks very much like a direct address, and is therefore further evidence that she was present for the hearing—that, should her complaints be found to be false, she would have an appropriately severe punishment as due warning to those bringing malicious claims against their enemies.[36]

In the event, this whole affair ended in something of a whitewash. Sir Richard Stanhope was rapidly released from prison and, after a brief appearance before the King's Bench at Shrewsbury, secured a general pardon that he deployed to secure release from all the charges recently brought in Parliament, including his alleged crimes against Margaret Basset.[37] He therefore held on to possession of those Basset properties that he had claimed as his own, and was later confirmed by the Crown to be in lawful possession of them.[38] Apart from showing the general difficulties that women of the landed class had in convincing the courts of the veracity of their claims against powerful men, the case is especially significant in demonstrating that, under certain exceptional circumstances, a woman might actually appear in person before the king and Lords in Parliament when they sat in deliberation of certain of the more intractable private petitions under their purview.

Conclusion

This review of petitions entered in Parliament by women of gentry and lesser standing indicates that, particularly under the first three Edwards, the social range of female petitioners could be very broad, including peasant women and those who were self-declared paupers. In the fifteenth century many of the poorer sort preferred to take their cases to Chancery rather than to Parliament, not because the latter had set itself against such business but simply because of the greater convenience involved in submitting a bill to the chancellor's court. The petition of Margaret Basset, while exceptional in its detail and its suggestion of the presence of the female petitioner at a hearing in Parliament, happens also to be generally illustrative of the fact that Parliament was, by the middle of the fifteenth century, dealing mainly with female petitioners who were members of landed society. The main interest of the petitions brought in Parliament by women of various degrees, however, lies in the way in which the supplicants sought to find ways around the normal restrictions of the common law and allow married women to petition in their own right. While this strategy was by no means always successful, the fact that the Crown did, under certain circumstances, allow married women their own voices in raising concerns within Parliament offers some quite powerful testimony of women's agency in parliamentary process. We shall see in Chaps. 6 and 7 how that agency also extended to other challenges to feudal and common law that gave women a role, albeit secondary, in the making or unmaking of statutory legislation.

Notes

1. Payling, 'Demographic Change', 54–6. See also Payling, 'Economics of Marriage', which argues (428–9) that 'heiress hunting' was more prevalent in the lower ranks of landed society than in the peerage.
2. SC 8/68/3378.
3. SC 8/11/541; SC 8/11/542; SC 8/33/1648; and SC 8/158/7861. The petition referring to the case in Parliament is SC 8/267/13319.
4. SC 8/77/3826; SC 8/80/3996; and SC 8/120/5988. Prior to her marriage to Veys, Catherine also petitioned in her own right: SC 8/36/1791.
5. SC 8/79/3904.
6. SC 8/83/4108A.
7. SC 8/52/2557, with detailed modern reasoning on the date provided on the guard of the document. Compare the petition of Agnes atte le Wode of Beoley (Worcestershire) who, in 1320, claimed to have sued out fourteen writs for the recovery of goods and beasts taken from her and her son, but all to no avail: SC 8/3/125, printed in *RP*, I, 365.
8. SC 8/244/12176. Because this petition was previously enclosed with the Chancery warrant C 81/330/19422, it can be associated with the Parliament of March 1348.
9. SC 8/124/6188A.
10. SC 8/110/5479.
11. SC 8/7/336, printed in *RP*, I, 415 and noted in *PROME*, III, 457. For discussion, see Harris, 'Taking Your Chances', 177; and Ormrod, 'Road to Boroughbridge', 82.
12. PRO 31/7/151, no. 60, transcribed and translated in *PROME*, II, 265, 336–7. For the 1303–1304 campaign, see Prestwich, *Edward I*, 498–502.
13. For similar strategies by men, see Dodd, *Justice and Grace*, 290–302.
14. SC 8/43/2103.
15. SC 8/69/3432.
16. SC 8/179/8929, printed in *RP*, II, 35, and noted in *PROME*, III, 460.
17. Butler, *Divorce in Medieval England*, 64 (where the Surdeval case discussed here is also cited).
18. See the case of Lucy de Latymer, whose petition stressed—twice—that her soul would be imperilled by returning to her husband, William, since the divorce had been brought because the couple were related within the prohibited degree. The church courts of York, however, warned the Crown

off interfering in the case: SC 8/324/E640-E641. In a petition of *c.* 1280, the plaintiff requested that the king require that his estranged wife be separated from her abductor-husband, but stressed that church law needed to prevail: SC 8/51/2520.

19. SC 8/275/13736, printed in Maitland, ed., *Memoranda de Parliamento*, 81–2, and transcribed and translated in *PROME*, II, 221, 291.
20. See below, 131. In the Parliament of 1449–1450 the Commons included in their petition for the property to be exempt from a new act of resumption a specific point about lands that may have been inherited overseas through alien women who married English men: *PROME*, XII, 110.
21. *PROME*, IX, 260; Ormrod, 'Enmity or Amity?', 28.
22. *PROME*, X, 162–4; XI, 133–4; Ormrod, Lambert and Mackman, *Immigrant England*, 210.
23. For petitions from husbands and wives jointly, see SC 8/26/1253; SC 8/26/1279, printed in *PROME*, XI, 117; SC 8/85/4230; and SC 8/85/4242. For petitions from women stating their married status but acting in their own right, see SC 8/25/1216, printed in *RP*, IV, 309; SC 8/85/4224; SC 8/85/4227; and SC 8/96/4794.
24. Ormrod, Lambert and Mackman, *Immigrant England*, 20.
25. 1431 petition: SC 8/26/1259, printed in *RP*, IV, 384, and dated by Biggs, 'Patronage, Preference and Survival', 157 n. 91.
26. SC 8/97/4807, printed in Rees, ed., *Calendar of Ancient Petitions Relating to Wales*, 151–2.
27. SC 8/97/4809, with pilgrimage proved by *CPR, 1330–4*, 80.
28. SC 8/101/5053. For similar petitions from wives in relation to husbands imprisoned in England, see SC 8/33/1645; SC 8/52/2586; SC 8/60/2994; SC 8/69/3432; and SC 8/127/6306. For two petitions relating to a case of a (presumably widowed) mother petitioning for the release of her son from prison, see SC 8/148/7371; and SC 8/149/7410.
29. SC 8/21/1018, printed in *RP*, III, 256. Thomas Felton also petitioned in person on the same matter: SC 8/111/5514; and Ambühl and Dodd, 'Politics of Surrender', 236–7. For other women's petitions referring to husbands as prisoners of war, see SC 8/21/1016, printed in *RP*, III, 256; and SC 8/70/3459, discussed below, 69.
30. For the background, see Powell, *Kingship, Law, and Society*, 169–94.
31. For what follows, see SC 8/97/4801. I am grateful to Jonathan Mackman for assistance with the text of this petition and its endorsement.
32. '[Richard,]... adonques esteant present devant le Roi et les seigneurs espirituelx et temperelx ...'. For further, unconnected, allegations against Stanhope registered at the Leicester Parliament, see SC 8/23/1128-9, printed in *RP*, IV, 29–30, and summarised in *PROME*, IX, 62.
33. Taylor, 'Chronicle of John Strecche', 147.

34. For which see Powell, *Kingship, Law, and Society*, 225.
35. 'pur ceo … qe mesme cely Richard fuit un de les pluis puissantz et riotous persones du dit countee & la dite Margarete fuit une poure & simple vewe …'.
36. 'Et outreceo le Roi disoit a dite Margarete qe si ses compleints ceste pertie soient trovez encontre luy qe adonques ele avera tiele punissement qe serra as autres cause et ensample de cesser enapres tieux mains verraiez suggestions affairez a sa roiale mageste.'
37. Powell, *Kingship, Law, and Society*, 227. Stanhope's petition for redress at the November 1414 Parliament is SC 8/23/1140, printed in *RP*, IV, 55–6.
38. Roskell, Clark and Rawcliffe, *House of Commons*, IV, 454. Stanhope's appeal on the case, submitted to Parliament in November 1414, is SC 8/23/1140, printed in *RP*, IV, 56, and noted in *PROME*, IX, 110.

References

Unpublished Primary Sources

Kew, The National Archives of the United Kingdom
C 81 Chancery: Warrants for the Great Seal, Series I.
PRO 31 Transcripts, General.
SC 8 Special Collections: Ancient Petitions.

Published Primary Sources

Brand, Paul, Seymour Phillips, W. Mark Ormrod, Geoffrey Martin, Chris Given Wilson, Anne Curry and Rosemary Horrox, eds, *The Parliament Rolls of Medieval England*, 16 vols (Woodbridge: Boydell, 2005).

Calendar of the Patent Rolls Preserved in the Public Record Office, Henry III–Henry VII, 54 vols (London: Her/His Majesty's Stationery Office, 1891–1916).

Maitland, Frederic W., ed., *Memoranda de Parliamento, 1305*, Rolls Series 98 (London, 1893).

Rees, William, ed., *Calendar of Ancient Petitions Relating to Wales* (Cardiff: University of Wales Press, 1975).

Strachey, J., ed., *Rotuli Parliamentorum*, 6 vols (London: Record Commission, 1767–1777).

Published Secondary Sources

Ambühl, Rémy and Gwilym Dodd, 'The Politics of Surrender: Treason, Trials and Recrimination in the 1370s', in *Ruling Fourteenth-Century England: Essays in Honour of Christopher Given-Wilson*, ed. Rémy Ambühl, James Bothwell and Laura Tompkins (Woodbridge: Boydell, 2019), 227–261.

Biggs, Douglas L., 'Patronage, Preference and Survival: The Life of Lady Margaret Sarnesfield, *c.* 1381–*c.* 1444', in *The Ties That Bind: Essays in Medieval British History in Honor of Barbara Hanawalt*, ed. Linda E. Mitchell, Katherine L. French and Douglas L. Biggs (Farnham: Ashgate, 2011), 143–58.

Butler, Sara M., *Divorce in Medieval England: From One to Two Persons in Law* (London: Routledge, 2013).

Dodd, Gwilym, *Justice and Grace: Private Petitioning and the English Parliament in the Late Middle Ages* (Oxford: Oxford University Press, 2007).

Harris, Simon J., 'Taking Your Chances: Petitioning in the Last Years of Edward II and the First Years of Edward III', in *Medieval Petitions: Grace and Grievance*, ed. W. Mark Ormrod, Gwilym Dodd and Anthony Musson (York: York Medieval Press, 2009), 173–92.

Ormrod, W. Mark, 'Enmity or Amity? The Status of French Immigrants to England during an Age of War, *c.* 1290–*c.* 1540', *History* 105 (2020).

Ormrod, W. Mark, 'The Road to Boroughbridge: The Civil War of 1321–2 in the Ancient Petitions', in *Foundations of Medieval Scholarship: Records Edited in Honour of David Crook*, ed. Paul Brand and Sean Cunningham (York: Borthwick Institute for Archives, 2008), 77–88.

Ormrod, W. Mark, Bart Lambert and Jonathan Mackman, *Immigrant England, 1300–1550* (Manchester: Manchester University Press, 2019).

Payling, Simon J., 'Demographic Change and Landed Society in Late Medieval England', *Economic History Review* 2nd ser. 45 (1992): 51–73.

Payling, Simon J., 'The Economics of Marriage in Late Medieval England: The Marriage of Heiresses', *Economic History Review* 2nd ser. 54 (2001): 413–29.

Powell, Edward, *Kingship, Law, and Society: Criminal Justice in the Reign of Henry V* (Oxford: Clarendon Press, 1989).

Prestwich, Michael, *Edward I* (London: Yale University Press, 1988).

Roskell, J. S., Linda Clark and Carole Rawcliffe, *The House of Commons, 1386–1421*, 4 vols (Stroud: Sutton, 1992).

Taylor, Frank, 'The Chronicle of John Strecche for the Reign of Henry V, 1414–1422', *Bulletin of the John Rylands Library* 16 (1932): 137–87.

CHAPTER 4

Women on Trial in Parliament

Abstract The only case in which a woman was put to trial in Parliament during the later Middle Ages was that of Alice Perrers, the mistress of Edward III. An analysis of this case reveals the deeply misogynistic attitude of Parliament towards women who dared to challenge the patriarchy by acting independently of male authority. Ironically, Alice's marriage to William Windsor, which she tried to use in order to extricate herself from the parliamentary judgment of 1377, proved disabling: the royal Council vested interest in Alice's former property not in the couple jointly but in the husband alone. The chapter concludes with a short analysis of the trial of Eleanor Cobham, duchess of Gloucester, in the fifteenth century, which was conducted not as a treason trial in Parliament but as a case of sorcery heard before an ecclesiastical court. Parliament was clearly uneasy about this, and secured a statute confirming that the wives of peers should, like their husbands, be tried before the Lords on charges of high crimes.

Keywords Gender • Justice • Law • Parliament

W. M. Ormrod, *Women and Parliament in Later Medieval England*, The New Middle Ages,
https://doi.org/10.1007/978-3-030-45220-9_4

Introduction

It was assumed in the later Middle Ages that women of high status who committed crimes when married to, or widowed from, members of the peerage might be subject to trial in Parliament.[1] In point of fact, however, women of the nobility who fell foul of the Crown were always tried and punished in their absence. The development in the fifteenth century of the act of attainder, a legislative process undertaken without the necessary presence or trial of the person(s) concerned, meant the imposition of the most brutal and stringent penalties in cases of treason and high crimes against the state. Royal and noble women who were subjected to such acts of attainder were not, however, put to death like their male counterparts, but were punished with perpetual imprisonment.[2] In reality, then, set-piece trials of noblewomen never actually took place in Parliament during the medieval period. For example, when Eleanor (née Beaufort), the widow of James Butler, earl of Wiltshire and Ormond, was declared attainted of high treason on the basis of her deceased husband's posthumous attainder in 1461, both she and the lands she held in jointure were simply put in the indefinite custody of one of Edward IV's most conspicuous supporters, John Wenlock.[3]

The Trials of Alice Perrers

There remains one instance, however, in which a woman—not in this case of the nobility, but actually from the commercial class of London—was subjected to a trial before the Lords in Parliament. This is the example of Alice Perrers, the widow of a London goldsmith who entered royal service as a waiting woman to Queen Philippa in the 1360s and became the mistress and constant companion of Edward III over the last decade of his life.[4] Alice was especially controversial for two reasons. First, she built up her own extensive portfolio of landed estates across southern and midland England, partly through royal patronage and partly by investing the large sums of money that she appears to have extracted from the personal wealth of Edward III.[5] Secondly and more unusually for a woman, she was deeply embroiled in the network of financiers that existed among the merchants of London and who took advantage of the Exchequer's impecuniousness in the 1370s to lend money to the ageing Edward III at punitive rates of interest. Alice did herself no favours: she clearly had an abrasive style that went down badly with many members of the court. But her modern rehabilitation from medieval misogyny credits her as a remarkable example of the *femme sole*, an independent businesswoman of talent and means who used her own social and political skills to develop a powerful circle of influence around Edward III during the ailing king's last years.[6]

The financial and political controversies created by that circle were, however, devastatingly exposed to public scrutiny in the so-called Good Parliament of 1376. This was the first Parliament in the Middle Ages to employ the process of impeachment, which involved a set of charges brought collectively by the Commons and heard by the Lords. A number of the male courtiers and financiers of Edward III were subjected to this process, including William Latimer, the chamberlain of the king's household, and Richard Lyons, a prominent London merchant with especially close ties to Alice Perrers. Alice herself was not put on trial, probably because John of Gaunt, the king's third son and effective president of this Parliament, was keen to avoid the scandal that might arise if the extent of her influence over Edward III was fully and publicly revealed. Instead, Perrers was spirited away from the king's side and made subject, in her absence, to an extraordinary parliamentary ordinance:

> Because a complaint was made to the king that some women have pursued various business and disputes in the king's courts by way of maintenance, bribing and influencing the parties, which thing displeases the king; the king forbids any woman to do it, and especially Alice Perrers, on penalty of whatever the said Alice can forfeit and of being banished from the realm.[7]

The threat that this ordinance posed—the disclosure of Perrers' nefarious manipulations of the law for personal gain—was enough to scare her off. Left in an untenable and highly precarious position, Alice was induced to abjure the court, in much the same way that Blanche, Lady Poynings, Joan, Lady Mohun and Eleanor, Lady Moleyns did later, in 1388, when the Lords Appellant conducted their great purge of Richard II's household.[8]

Matters did not end there for Alice Perrers, however. Once the immediate political crisis of 1376 was over, Edward III rapidly recalled his mistress to his side, and over the winter of 1376–1377 Alice recovered most of the lands and goods that she had accumulated under Edward's patronage during their liaison. As a result, in the first Parliament to be held after Edward III's death in October 1377, there was significant clamour from the Commons for Alice to be put to a further, full-scale parliamentary trial.[9] Richard II's minority administration, run by Gaunt, reluctantly bowed to pressure and, at the end of the assembly, brought Alice into Parliament to answer a series of major political charges.[10] In addition, all those wishing to sue her in a private capacity were encouraged to submit petitions under a proclamation announced in the city of London.[11] Although Parliament was formally dissolved before Perrers' trial was concluded, most of the Commons seem to have remained in the capital to observe the spectacle and did not go down until after the final judgment was given on 3 December.[12] One by one, members of the court of Edward III lined up to confirm the charges against the former king's mistress: in particular, that Perrers had countermanded the Council's order that Sir Nicholas Dagworth be sent to Ireland; and that she had persuaded Edward III to show renewed favour to Richard Lyons, who had been condemned in the Good Parliament but pardoned and restored in the interim. Alice was declared guilty of all charges. Her punishment was to be perpetual banishment from the realm, with all her property confiscated to the Crown. The trial of 1377 therefore resulted in a re-affirmation of the ordinance of 1376 and the full—and apparently final—forfeiture of Perrers' considerable landed estate.

In the next Parliament to meet, the assembly that convened at Gloucester in October 1378, some forty petitions were received in response to the 1377 call for private suits against the former king's mistress, revealing Alice's alleged interference in the workings of the courts for personal gain, her unscrupulous property transactions and her persistent disinclination to pay her debts. A number of these petitions were submitted by women acting as *femmes soles* or in conjunction with husbands: these include the petition of Princess Isabella, countess of Bedford, discussed in Chap. 2, and a notable petition from Robert Lucas, another London goldsmith, and his wife Margaret, who complained that Perrers had reneged on her promise to pay the debts owed to Edward III and Queen Philippa by Margaret's first husband.[13] Other petitions, from men of various classes, complained of the way in which Alice had brought her influence to bear in the courts such as to block any proceedings they might take against her. Robert Osprynge of London claimed that gold and silver had been worthless when confronted with Alice's influence in the course of justice.[14]

Ironically, however, this body of private petitions had mostly to be set aside by the royal Council when it was discovered that Alice Perrers had—probably during her period of disgrace in 1376—undertaken a clandestine marriage with Sir William Windsor, Edward III's former lieutenant of Ireland. Windsor and Alice submitted a joint petition as husband and wife in the Gloucester Parliament, complaining of various procedural errors in Perrers' trial of 1377. Most seriously and substantively, they reported that they had already been married at the time of that trial. The presumption that Alice, widowed from her first husband, had been put to answer as *femme sole* was therefore false, and the judgment against her should be nullified.[15] In the end, Windsor did not press his case and preferred the arts of compromise: he reached an informal accommodation with the Council, which allowed him to take over the majority of his wife's former landed property, but which left her still technically subject to the judgment of 1377. The result was that Alice was doubly compromised, first by her marriage and secondly by her husband's desire to have complete control of her property and dispose of it to the benefit of his own relatives.[16] Alice remained trapped in this anomalous position until Windsor's death in 1384, at which point she was able, once again as *femme sole*, to petition in Parliament for the annulment of the 1377 judgment and the restoration of her estate.[17] Even this, however, did not end Alice's difficulties, since it proved remarkably difficult to wrest back control of a number of her most valuable properties; and for the rest of her widowhood, Perrers continued assiduously to petition in Parliament for the restoration of her rights.

The reluctance of the Crown to proceed against Alice Perrers in 1376 and 1377, and then to unravel the mess of the 1377 trial in addressing her continued grievances after 1384, says much about the patriarchal nature of the medieval English Parliament. Alice was not simply an embarrassment to the family of her former lover, Edward III. She also represented a wider challenge to the rule of men by exemplifying what an ambitious woman could achieve under the status of *femme sole*. In his second and third recensions of the epic dream poem, *Piers Plowman*, the writer William Langland adapted his rendition of the figure of Lady Mede, the personification of venality, to reflect some of the details of Alice Perrers' own tumultuous career and the trials of 1377 and 1378.[18] That the reverberations of these events were still being felt at the time of Alice's death in 1404 indicates just how ill equipped was the world of parliamentary politics for dealing with independently minded women who refused the normal conventions of marriage and widowhood. In this sense, Alice stands with some of the female petitioners we shall meet in Chaps. 6 and 7, who were prepared to challenge the normative view of women as meek and compliant in order to press their personal rights and interests as maidens, wives and widows.

The Trial of Eleanor Cobham

Apart from the trials of Alice Perrers, there are no cases in the later Middle Ages where a woman of any status was brought to formal judgment within the jurisdiction of Parliament. There was one further case heard outside Parliament, however, in which the Commons took some retrospective interest. In 1440–1441, Eleanor (née Cobham), the former mistress and now wife of Henry VI's uncle Humphrey, duke of Gloucester, was alleged to have consulted astrologers on the question of the royal succession.[19] Eleanor had seemingly developed a strong interest in the candidature of her husband to succeed the childless king, and under these circumstances the resort to astrology was deemed potentially treasonous. This, at least, was how various courtiers chose to interpret such activity in their wider aim of criticising and undermining the political influence of Duke Humphrey in the king's Council. Rumours began to develop in London, and the authorities reacted fast and arrested a number of Eleanor's advisers. When these men were charged with necromancy and heresy, Eleanor fled into sanctuary at Westminster Abbey. In spite of the Council's continued interest in the case, Eleanor herself insisted on being tried by the ecclesiastical authorities—not least because the church courts did not impose capital penalties. Before a panel of bishops, she declared herself innocent of most charges, but admitted procuring potions from Margery Jourdemayne, the so-called Witch of Eye, to help her bear children (and therefore royal heirs) to Duke Humphrey.[20] While her accomplices were put to death (Margery was burned as a witch), Eleanor was subjected by the ecclesiastical court to the lesser punishment of a public act of penance followed by perpetual imprisonment. For the rest of her life she languished in a series of royal prisons, eventually dying at Beaumaris Castle in 1452. Today, Duchess Eleanor's trial and condemnation are generally seen as part of a backlash against the political ambitions of her husband: her own culpability is regarded as merely marginal. At the time, however, the case had the same kind of sensational aspects as the trials of Alice Perrers, and like those earlier events was driven by a deeply misogynistic political culture.

Eleanor Cobham was not the only high-status woman to be accused of treasonous necromancy in the fifteenth century. In 1419 Joan of Navarre, the widow of King Henry IV, had been imprisoned—though never formally charged and tried—on suspicion of plotting Henry V's death by sorcery and witchcraft.[21] What makes the trial of Cobham interesting and unique in the present context, however, is the response to her trial in the Parliament of 1442. There was evidently some concern that Eleanor had been allowed to get away with judgment before an ecclesiastical tribunal on charges that had included treason. The Commons now demanded that the wives and widows of peers 'shall be brought to answer and put to answer and judged before the same judges and peers of the realm as are other [male] peers of the realm, if they should be indicted or impeached of such treasons or felonies committed or later to be committed'.[22] On the one hand, the resulting statute re-asserted the special right of all peers (and now, their wives) to have major charges against them heard by proper judicial process before the Lords in Parliament, thus avoiding the kangaroo courts that had sometimes delivered arbitrary judgments of treason in the fourteenth century. On the other hand, and in the spirit of the moment, the legislation reflected a concern to bring noblewomen within the terms of existing legislation relating to their menfolk and to insist that acts of treason by people of aristocratic status be subject to the definitive jurisdiction of the highest secular court in the land. In practice, the statute of 1442 had no direct effect on the way that fifteenth-century noblewomen were treated: the process involved in acts of attainder, which were by now the norm for cases of treason, meant that neither male nor female defendants were allowed to appear and make their case before the court of Parliament. The 1442 legislation remains interesting, however, in terms of the vigilance that Parliament imagined to exercise over its own jurisdiction and the eagerness with which the Commons asserted the control that the institution ought to have over the offences of high-status women.

Notes

1. See below, 59.
2. Seabourne, *Imprisoning Medieval Women*, 30–3.
3. *CPR, 1461–7*, 178, cited by Rosenthal, 'Other Victims', 223. For the attainder of James Butler, see C 65/106, m. 12–13, printed in *RP*, V, 480–2, and in *PROME*, XIII, 49–55. For Eleanor Beaufort, see Cokayne, *Complete Peerage*, X, 128–9; and for Wenlock, see Kekewich, 'Wenlock, John, first Baron Wenlock', 110–11.
4. For the full details of this case, see Ormrod, 'Trials of Alice Perrers'. For Alice's first husband, see Tompkins, 'Alice Perrers and the Goldsmiths' Mistery'.
5. Bothwell, 'Management of Position'.

6. Trigg, 'Traffic in Medieval Women'; Mortimer, *The Perfect King*, 378–82.
7. C 65/30, m. 7, printed in *RP*, II, 329, and in *PROME*, V, 313: 'Pur ce qe pleinte est faite au roy qe aucuns femmes ont pursuys en les courtz du roi diverses busoignes et quereles par voie de maintenance, et pur lower et part avoir, quele chose desplest au roi; et le roi defende qe desormes nulle femme le face, et par especial Alice Perers, sur peine de quanqe la dite Alice purra forfaire, et d'estre bannitz hors du roialme.'
8. Hector and Harvey, eds, *Westminster Chronicle*, 231. This was an imitation of the formal process of abjuration by which those indicted of capital offences could be quit of the charges on condition that they leave the realm, never to return. See Jordan, *From England to France*.
9. C 65/32, m. 8, printed in *RP*, III, 14, and in *PROME*, VI, 30, 31.
10. C 65/32, m. 7, printed in *RP*, 12–14, and in *PROME*, VI, 26–30.
11. *CCR, 1377–81*, 112, summarised in *PROME*, VI, 65; and Sharpe, ed., *Calendar of the Letter Books of the City of London*, VIII (Letter Book H), 81.
12. Ormrod, 'Trials of Alice Perrers', 375–9.
13. SC 8/129/6449.
14. SC 8/103/5132.
15. SC 8/18/890, summarised in *PROME*, VI, 87–8; and SC 8/146/7279.
16. Gambier-Parry, 'Alice Perrers and her Husband's Relatives'.
17. *PROME*, VI, 388–9.
18. Giancarlo, '*Piers Plowman*, Parliament, and the Public Voice'.
19. For what follows, see Griffiths, 'Trial of Eleanor Cobham'; Carey, *Courting Disaster*, 138–53.
20. For further details, see Freeman, 'Sorcery at Court and Manor'.
21. Myers, *Crown, Household and Parliament*, 93–134.
22. C 49/25/6, enrolled on the parliament at C 65/96, m. 5, printed from the latter in *RP*, V, 56, and in *PROME*, XI, 367–8, and leading to the legislation in *SR*, II, 321–2: '… soient menez en respoundre, et mys a responder et adjuggez, devaunt tielx juges et peres de la roialme, si come autres peres de le roialme serroient, s'ils fuissent enditez ou empeschez de tielx tresons out felonies faitz, ou en apres affairez.' See also Bellamy, *Law of Treason*, 154.

References

Unpublished Primary Sources

Kew, The National Archives of the United Kingdom
C 49 Chancery and Exchequer: King's Remembrancer: Parliamentary and Council Proceedings.

C 65 Chancery: Parliament Rolls.
SC 8 Special Collections: Ancient Petitions.

Published Primary Sources

Brand, Paul, Seymour Phillips, W. Mark Ormrod, Geoffrey Martin, Chris Given Wilson, Anne Curry and Rosemary Horrox, eds, *The Parliament Rolls of Medieval England*, 16 vols (Woodbridge: Boydell, 2005).

Calendar of the Close Rolls Preserved in the Public Record Office, Henry III-Henry VII, 61 vols (London: Her/His Majesty's Stationery Office, 1892–1963).

Calendar of the Patent Rolls Preserved in the Public Record Office, Henry III–Henry VII, 54 vols (London: Her/His Majesty's Stationery Office, 1891–1916).

Hector, L. C. and Barbara F. Harvey, eds, *The Westminster Chronicle, 1381–1394* (Oxford: Clarendon Press, 1982).

Raithby, John, ed., *The Statutes of the Realm*, 11 vols (London: Record Commission, 1810–1828).

Sharpe, Reginald R., ed., *Calendar of the Letter Books of the City of London*, 12 vols (London: Her/His Majesty's Stationery Office, 1899–1912).

Strachey, J., ed., *Rotuli Parliamentorum*, 6 vols (London: Record Commission, 1767–1777).

Published Secondary Sources

Bellamy, J. G., *The Law of Treason in England in the Later Middle Ages* (Cambridge: Cambridge University Press, 1970).

Bothwell, James, 'The Management of Position: Alice Perrers, Edward III, and the Creation of a Landed Estate, 1362–1377', *Journal of Medieval History* 24 (1998): 31–51.

Carey, Hilary M., *Courting Disaster: Astrology at the English Court and University in the Later Middle Ages* (Basingstoke: Macmillan, 1991).

Cokayne, G. E., *The Complete Peerage*, rev. edn, 13 vols (London, 1910–1959).

Freeman, Jessica, 'Sorcery at Court and Manor: Margery Jourdemayne, the Witch of Eye next Westminster', *Journal of Medieval History* 30 (2004): 343–57.

Gambier-Parry, T. R., 'Alice Perrers and her Husband's Relatives', *English Historical Review* 47 (1932): 272–6.

Giancarlo, Matthew, '*Piers Plowman*, Parliament, and the Public Voice', *Yearbook of Langland Studies* 17 (2003): 135–74.

Griffiths, Ralph A., 'The Trial of Eleanor Cobham: An Episode in the Fall of Duke Humphrey of Gloucester', *Bulletin of the John Rylands Library* 51 (1968–1969): 381–99.

Jordan, William Chester, *From England to France: Felony and Exile in the High Middle Ages* (Princeton: Princeton University Press, 2015).

Kekewich, Margaret L., 'Wenlock, John, first Baron Wenlock', in H. C. G. Matthew and Brian H. Harrison, eds, *The Oxford Dictionary of National Biography*, 60 vols (Oxford: Oxford University Press, 2004), LVIII, 110–11.

Mortimer, Ian, *The Perfect King: The Life of Edward III, Father of the English Nation* (London: Vintage, 2006).

Myers, A. R., *Crown, Household and Parliament in Fifteenth-Century England* (London: Hambledon, 1985).

Ormrod, W. Mark, 'The Trials of Alice Perrers', *Speculum* 83 (2008): 366–96.

Rosenthal, Joel T., 'Other Victims: Peeresses as War Widows, 1450–1500', *History* 72 (1987): 213–30.

Seabourne, Gwen, *Imprisoning Medieval Women: The Non-Judicial Confinement and Abduction of Women in England, c. 1170–1509* (Farnham: Ashgate, 2011).

Tompkins, Laura, 'Alice Perrers and the Goldsmiths' Mistery: New Evidence Concerning the Identity of the Mistress of Edward III', *English Historical Review* 130 (2015): 1361–91.

Trigg, Stephanie, 'The Traffic in Medieval Women: Alice Perrers, Feminist Critics, and *Piers Plowman*', *Yearbook of Langland Studies* 12 (1998): 5–29.

CHAPTER 5

Female Institutions and Collectives as Petitioners in Parliament

Abstract Women had fewer opportunities than men to petition in Parliament as collectives, but there are instances across the later Middle Ages in which they did so. An important category in this respect comprises petitions submitted by houses of nuns. Sometimes, nuns tried to petition as individuals, but since the Crown did not recognise religious as having individual identities, they could only do so successfully as corporate bodies, making their supplications in the name of the entire house. Petitions from nuns were dominated by pleas of poverty. Among instances of groups of laywomen acting corporately, a series of petitions from the London silkwomen across the second half of the fifteenth century earns special analysis. Other 'imagined' communities including named or unnamed women are assessed in order to evaluate the degree of female agency that are represented in the business they put forward through their petitions.

Keywords Collectives • Gender • Nunneries • Nuns • Parliament • Silkwomen • Widows

W. M. Ormrod, *Women and Parliament in Later Medieval England*, The New Middle Ages,
https://doi.org/10.1007/978-3-030-45220-9_5

Introduction

Although women had many fewer opportunities for collective action than did men in the later Middle Ages, they nonetheless sometimes petitioned in Parliament in formal or informal groups. This category of parliamentary petition is interesting and rewarding, as it reflects the ways in which women imagined themselves as members of wider social or institutional orders and considered it their right to supplicate in the name of the entire collective.

Nuns as Petitioners in Parliament

The most stable and constant of these collectives were female religious houses, which, as Table 1.1 shows, account for 77 instances, or 1%, of the total number of cases in the 'Parliamentary Petitions' section of the Ancient Petitions.[1] It may be that communities of nuns were disposed to petition in Parliament because this was the one royal assembly that formally included a number of heads of male religious houses summoned, along with the bishops of the realm, to sit in the Lords. The 'mitred abbots', as this group are sometimes called, were keen to express their independence from secular obligations and were often represented in Parliament by their proctors; but these, not infrequently drawn from the clerical elites in central government, were themselves adept at the intricacies of parliamentary process and may have felt a responsibility to press the cases of the religious orders more generally.[2]

It is worth noting, however, that the master of Sempringham, the male head of the mixed religious order of nuns and canons known as the Gilbertines, secured exemption from attendance at Parliament in 1343, along with a number of heads of male Benedictine houses.[3] This meant that the only direct representation of female religious (by a male head of the order) in Parliament ceased from this point. It may be instructive that the only petition from the Gilbertines as an entire order known to have been submitted in Parliament dates from before the withdrawal of the order's master: it came in 1307, when the order of Sempringham requested assistance towards the upkeep of the wives and daughters of the king's Scottish enemies who had been placed in various of their houses for safe custody.[4] Edward I's wars in Wales and Scotland had resulted in the capture of a number of high-status women who were brought back to England and accorded varying degrees of comfort: Gwenllian, daughter of Llewelyn ap Gruffudd, prince of Wales, resided in honourable estate at the Gilbertines' mother house of Sempringham for some fifty years.[5] A later petition (*c.* 1383) from the 'master, priors and nuns' of the Gilbertines also survives, but this address was a mere flourish ahead of the naming of the real group concerned, the nuns of a single house within the order at Watton (East Riding of Yorkshire).[6]

Very occasionally, other groupings of nuns also operated at a macro-level, involving the whole of their own order and even others. In one case, early in the reign of Edward III, a petition was presented in Parliament in the name of 'his poor nuns, the abbesses and prioresses' (*ses povres non-eynes abbesses et prioresses*) of the entire province of Canterbury, requesting the king's support against bishops who charged fees for the admission of new nuns beyond the established number in each house.[7] In this instance we are invited to imagine collaboration between the heads of female religious houses across a number of orders in pursuit of what they regarded as a common grievance. In reality, the petition may have been prompted by the grievances of one nunnery, or perhaps several within a particular diocese; under these circumstances, it may have been simply 'dressed up' to make the complaint look more common than it really was.

Generally, petitions sent to Parliament in this category came from individual nunneries, and were made in the name of the abbess/prioress and sisters of the named house. In a single case, we have a petition from a named nun in a given convent, when Mary de Preston, a religious of the Benedictine convent at Wilberfoss (East Riding of Yorkshire), complained during the reign of Edward II about the refusal of her kinsman, Gerard Salvayn, to pay rent for lands of hers that had been leased to him on her admission to the nunnery. The royal response was punctilious, stressing that the resulting action against Salvayn needed to be made in the name of prioress and convent of Wilberfoss, since all Mary's property was deemed by law to be part of the common possessions of the house. Mary Preston had clearly been badly advised and supported by the male paralegal who presumably drew up her petition.[8]

Petitions from female religious were dominated by the physical and economic conditions of their convents. There are frequent requests for confirmation of existing grants of land and for licences to acquire additional property. In 1330, the abbess and convent of the Augustinian house at Canonsleigh in Devon reported a long-standing grievance that the considerable sum of £672 given to them by Maud de Clare, countess of Gloucester (d. 1289), their foundress, had been confiscated by Edward I and that throughout the reign of Edward II the Crown had failed to provide them with any effective recompense.[9] And in 1432, the royal foundation of Brigittine nuns at Syon (Middlesex) requested confirmation of the royal letters patent on which basis they had moved their house from its original position to a new site downstream on the Thames in the manor and parish of Isleworth.[10]

Among the more adamant female religious houses petitioning the Crown in Parliament were others that claimed a royal foundation. The Benedictine nuns of Godstow (Oxfordshire), for example, petitioned on several occasions in the late thirteenth and fourteenth centuries for the fulfilment and upholding of their ancient rights, many of which they claimed to have been granted by royal charter, as well as for licences to acquire new property.[11] Others requested support because the property at issue had been granted by the king. In the early 1330s, for example, the abbess of the house of Augustinian nuns at Burnham (Buckinghamshire) petitioned against Geoffrey de Bulstrode, who had occupied lands previously leased to the convent by the Crown; on one of these occasions the abbess specifically requested that Bulstrode be brought into Parliament to answer the charges against him.[12]

By the same token, pleas of poverty were particularly prevalent among petitions from female religious houses (like male ones) made in Parliament.[13] In 1334, for example, the nuns of the Benedictine house at Cannington (Somerset) indicated that they could not afford to hire their own priest to say mass, but were dependent on the local parish priest for his services; they gratefully acknowledged that one of their patrons, Robert FitzPayn, was prepared to make a donation of land to the house that could be used to resource a chaplain for them, and wished the king's good favour in making this be so.[14] And in 1382, the abbess and convent of the royal foundation of Benedictine nuns at Shaftesbury (Dorset) petitioned in Parliament to have their entire estate taken under royal protection because plagues among people and murrains among cattle had left them virtually destitute and unable to pay their creditors.[15] The fact that female religious houses were generally poorer than male ones, and often existed in a state of affected or real penury, was used to add general force to the request for royal intervention. In 1338, the Council remarked in its endorsement to a petition from the prioress and nuns of the Benedictine house at Little Marlow (Berkshire) that the sisters should have their request for further resources supported because 'they are poor, and of good condition' (*elles sont povres et de bone condicion*).[16]

Lay Female Collectives as Petitioners in Parliament

More interesting in terms of the ingenuity involved in the submission of women's petitions are those that claimed to be made in the name of a formal or imagined collective of lay women. One well-known example is the series of petitions lodged in Parliament during the second half of the fifteenth century by the silkwomen of London, who (unusually) enjoyed something akin to the corporate status accorded to other, male, craft guilds in the city. The petitions of the silkwomen are especially important in the development of a parliamentary rhetoric, emerging during the second half of the fifteenth century, that saw alien craftspeople as a direct threat to traditional English trades and aimed, through royal legislation, to restrict the rights of foreign artisans entering the kingdom.[17] In their first petition, in 1455, for example, the silkwomen expressed clearly both their sense of status and their hostility to foreigners:

> The silkwomen and spinners of the crafts and occupations of silkworking in the city of London, which have been the crafts of women within the same city from time out of mind, ... pray and beseech that it is pleasing to God that all his creatures should be placed in virtuous employment and work according to their degree .... [But] recently various Lombards and other alien foreigners, planning to destroy the same crafts and all such virtuous occupations for women within the land, with the intention of enriching themselves and placing such occupations in other lands, now bring daily into this land manufactured silk, spun ribbons and laces, falsely and deceitfully made ....[18]

A good deal less remarked than the petitions of the silkwomen are a number of petitions claiming to speak in the name of the women of London as a generalised entity. Early in the reign of Edward III, for example, 'the poor women of London' (*les peuvres femmes de Loundres*) petitioned for the repayment of debts owed to them by the king's father. Tellingly, the response stated that the women concerned would have to identify themselves, and the details of the relevant debts, before the matter could proceed further.[19] In this case, a 'corporate' approach was rebuffed and the Crown accepted liability only if individual creditors made themselves known.

Questions about the success or originality of female collective agency also arise in relation to a petition of 1394 made in the name of 'your humble and poor oratrices, the widows of London' (*voz humbles et poures oratrices les veues de Londres*), requesting confirmation of the exemption they demanded, of right, from a levy being made in the capital to pay off the fine that Richard II had imposed as a consequence of a dispute with the city authorities in 1392.[20] An almost identical petition (though not in the same hand), claiming the same exemption, was submitted at the same time by 'your poor orators, the people of Holy Church in London and its suburbs' (*voz poures oratores, les gentz de Seinte Eglise deinz la cite de Londres et les suburbes dycelles*).[21] Both of these petitions appear to be conscious reactions to a third petition, made by the mayor, aldermen and commonalty of London, demanding that the Crown declare churchmen and widows to be liable to the special levy.[22] It seems, then, that the petition of the 'widows of London' may have been the creation of the clerical authorities, or of other male groupings interested in challenging the collection of the fine, rather than arising spontaneously from an identifiable pressure group representing widowed women as a group within the capital.

To deny the women of London any influence or interest in these or other issues is, however, inappropriate. In an early fourteenth-century petition that may have been presented in the Parliament of 1316, 'both [the] widows of the city of London and other women of the land' (*veues ausibien de la cite de Loundres et autres femmes de la terre*) requested relief for widows wishing to claim damages for dower property withheld from them after the deaths of their husbands, under the provision for this matter made in the Statute of Merton (1235). Because the statute had not specifically applied this measure to London, the petitioners argued that widows there were being deprived of this right under the custom of the city and were consequently finding it impossible to recover both the disputed property and the damages due.[23] In this instance, there is no extant companion petition from any male collective. That the petition deals with the law of dower is no doubt significant: as we shall see in Chap. 6, dower was one of the most regular issues on which independent women submitted private petitions to Parliament. We are therefore left with the intriguing possibility that the women of London, and more particularly London widows, did indeed have some means by which they could articulate common concerns in Parliament.

These examples of petitions made in the collective name of women are, however, highly unusual. Their rarity stands as testimony to the fact that women did not attend the local courts of the town, city, hundred and shire and were not considered to have a direct voice in meetings of the guilds and fraternities run by their menfolk in many incorporated towns. This is not to suppose that women could not be part of 'imagined' collectives.[24] The Ancient Petitions series is full of petitions registered in the name of real or fictional groups. Merchants petitioning in Parliament habitually inflated the urgency of their grievance by claiming to act in the name of '[all the] merchants of the realm', while those who were members of the shire elites frequently co-opted the notion of the 'county community' to give their petitions further force.[25] In exceptional circumstances, women could be named as part of such imagined collectives. One tantalising glimpse of female agency in this regard is provided by the formal inclusion, in a petition of 1422, of the dowager countess of Cambridge and the dowager Lady Deincourt, along with John, Lord Talbot and four named knights and esquires, the urban communities of York and Hull and the county community of Yorkshire. The petition expressed concern at the blocking of an important watercourse, and requested instructions requiring the re-modelling of a bridge in order to allow river transport to pass unimpeded.[26] In this instance, it is likely that the matter had been discussed at the Yorkshire county court, where the two noblewomen would have been represented by their stewards. Importantly, however, the petition stated that all the named individuals and communities were prepared to contribute either to the widening of the bridge or to the construction of a drawbridge, like the one (they said) on London Bridge. The countess of Cambridge and Lady Deincourt were seemingly deemed active petitioners because they held estates in the relevant area and had already given their consent to participating in a programme of public works.[27] Apart from the instances from London cited above, however, the only other known petition from an *ad hoc* group of women submitted in Parliament is one made by the six wives (unnamed) of men who had stood as hostages for the ransom of 1000 marks (£667) offered by the community of Ripon at the time of the serious Scottish incursion into Yorkshire in 1318.[28]

The general absence of petitions from informally constituted collectives of women is especially important in understanding the routes by which women's issues got taken up by Parliament when, from the later fourteenth century, the Commons began to 'avow' or adopt private petitions and include them in the schedule of common petitions submitted to the king and Council.[29] Petitions from county communities and urban corporations expressed a *prima facie* 'commonness' that increased the chances of the matter being taken up by the Commons in a given assembly.[30] Women's voices, however, were almost never raised in similar collective action. Rather, women had to rely either on the force of their own individual arguments, or on the awareness of the men who sat in the Commons about some general matter relating to women, in order to have their concerns taken forward in the common petitions and made into national legislation.

While all of this undoubtedly means that it was more difficult to have women's issues brought forward as public business in Parliament, it does not mean that the men who sat in Parliament were entirely blind to general concerns relating to women. Two issues in particular stand out here: dower, the portion of the husband's estate allowed to his wife as a life interest if he predeceased her; and rape, a term that included both the act of non-consensual sex and the crime of abduction. We shall continue this analysis of women and Parliament by examining these two themes in detail in the next two chapters, attempting in particular to analyse the degree of female agency in bringing about changes to the law during the later Middle Ages.

Notes

1. Six petitions from this section of the Ancient Petitions have recently been published *in extenso* in Dodd and McHardy, eds, *Petitions to the Crown from English Religious Houses*, 82, 89–90, 95–6, 100–1, 143–5, 189–90. Makowski, *English Nuns and the Law*, does not employ material from the Ancient Petitions.
2. Bradford and McHardy, eds, *Proctors for Parliament*, I, xii, xxvii–xxviii, xxxix–xlv.
3. Bradford and McHardy, eds, *Proctors for Parliament*, I, xxxix.
4. SC 8/71/3546, resulting in C 81/1538/8 and *CPR, 1301–7*, 503. SC 8/74/3667 (1334) and SC 8/140/6959 (1305) are addressed by the prior of Sempringham and refer only to the interests of the head house of the order.
5. Smith, *Llywelyn ap Gruffudd*, 579–80.
6. SC 8/140/6952.
7. SC 8/104/5191, published (with incorrect reference number) by Spear, 'Canterbury Lament'.
8. SC 8/66/3292.
9. SC 8/97/4839.
10. SC 8/26/1257A, transcribed on the parliament roll at C 65/91, m. 10, and printed from there in *RP*, IV, 395–6, and in *PROME*, XI, 23–5.

11. SC 8/16/774; SC 8/50/2473; SC 8/114/5660; and SC 8/114/5667, summarised in *PROME*, I, 42.
12. SC 8/97/4827; and SC 8/97/4828. For the background, reconstructed from printed sources, see Page, ed., *Victoria County History of Buckinghamshire*, I, 382.
13. See, for example, SC 8/61/3009; SC 8/83/4107, printed in Fraser, ed., *Ancient Petitions Relating to Northumberland*, 187; SC 8/142/7085; SC 8/164/8163; and SC 8/315/E193.
14. SC 8/54/2684, resulting in C 143/221/13 and *CPR, 1330–4*, 394.
15. SC 8/20/954, printed in Dodd and McHardy, eds, *Petitions to the Crown from English Religious Houses*, 100–1. For a similar case made by the nuns of Henwood (Warwickshire) in 1411, see SC 8/53/2635, resulting in C 81/651/6900 and *CPR, 1408–13*, 294–5.
16. SC 8/61/3009, resulting in *CPR, 1334–8*, 118.
17. Dale, 'London Silkwomen'; and Ormrod, Lambert and Mackman, *Immigrant England*, 33. See also Sutton, 'Two Dozen and More Silkwomen'; Brouquet, 'Girls at Work', 17–18.
18. SC 8/29/1410 (in Middle English), enrolled on the parliament roll at C 65/103, m. 2, and printed from the latter in *RP*, V, 325, and in *PROME*, XII, 438–9.
19. SC 8/120/5983.
20. SC 8/147/7343, printed from the original in *RP*, III, 325 and summarised in *PROME*, VII, 280. For the background, see Barron, 'Quarrel of Richard II'.
21. SC 8/22/1052, printed in *RP*, III, 325 and summarised in *PROME*, VII, 280.
22. SC 8/121/6036, printed in *RP*, III, 325, and summarised in *PROME*, VII, 280.
23. SC 8/346/E1388. The petition is endorsed 'before the Great Council' (*coram magno concilio*). For the statute, see *SR*, I, 1.
24. For the notion of 'imagined communities', see Johnson, 'Imagining Communities'.
25. Ormrod, 'Origins of Tunnage and Poundage, 220–6; Dodd, 'County and Community'.
26. SC 8/27/1330, discussed by Dodd, *Justice and Grace*, 212–13.
27. For the concern of another noblewoman, Joan (née FitzAlan), countess of Hereford, over her rights and those of her tenants with regard to charges on the bridge at Huntingdon, see SC 8/68/3368, printed in *RP*, III, 30, and summarised and dated to 1377 in *PROME*, V, 428, with reference to *CCR, 1374–7*, 523.
28. SC 8/70/3459. That the six husbands were also considered a collective is demonstrated by the subsequent petition of three of them, which notes

that they had been released (but had been required to leave their wives and children in their place) and that the other three had escaped from captivity: SC 8/89/4438. See also *CCR, 1318–23*, 274; *CIM*, II, no. 452.
29. For this development, see Dodd, *Justice and Grace*, 166–87.
30. Dodd, *Justice and Grace*, 242–78.

References

Unpublished Primary Sources

Kew, The National Archives of the United Kingdom
C 65 Chancery: Parliament Rolls.
C 81 Chancery: Warrants for the Great Seal, Series I.
C 143 Chancery: Inquisitions Ad Quod Dampnum, Henry III to Richard III.
SC 8 Special Collections: Ancient Petitions.

Published Primary Sources

Bradford, Phil, and Alison K. McHardy, eds, *Proctors for Parliament: Clergy, Community and Politics, c. 1248–1539*, 2 vols, Canterbury and York Society 107–8 (Woodbridge, 2017–2018).
Brand, Paul, Seymour Phillips, W. Mark Ormrod, Geoffrey Martin, Chris Given Wilson, Anne Curry and Rosemary Horrox, eds, *The Parliament Rolls of Medieval England*, 16 vols (Woodbridge: Boydell, 2005).
Calendar of the Close Rolls Preserved in the Public Record Office, Henry III-Henry VII, 61 vols (London: Her/His Majesty's Stationery Office, 1892–1963).
Calendar of Inquisitions Miscellaneous, 1219–1485, 8 vols (London/Woodbridge: His/Her Majesty's Stationery Office/Boydell, 1916–2003).
Calendar of the Patent Rolls Preserved in the Public Record Office, Henry III–Henry VII, 54 vols (London: Her/His Majesty's Stationery Office, 1891–1916).
Dodd, Gwilym and Alison K. McHardy, eds, *Petitions to the Crown from English Religious Houses, c. 1272–c. 1485*, Canterbury and York Society 100 (Woodbridge, 2010).
Fraser, Constance M., ed., *Ancient Petitions Relating to Northumberland*, Surtees Society 171 (Gateshead, 1961).
Raithby, John, ed., *The Statutes of the Realm*, 11 vols (London: Record Commission, 1810–1828).
Strachey, J., ed., *Rotuli Parliamentorum*, 6 vols (London: Record Commission, 1767–1777).

Published Secondary Sources

Barron, Caroline M., 'The Quarrel of Richard II with London, 1392–7', in *The Reign of Richard II: Essays in Honour of May McKisack*, ed. F. R. H. Du Boulay and Caroline M. Barron (London: Athlone Press, 1971), 173–201.

Dale, M. K., 'The London Silkwomen of the Fifteenth Century', *Economic History Review* 2nd ser. 4 (1932–1934): 324–35.

Dodd, Gwilym, 'County and Community in Medieval England', *English Historical Review* 134 (2019): 777–820.

Dodd, Gwilym, *Justice and Grace: Private Petitioning and the English Parliament in the Late Middle Ages* (Oxford: Oxford University Press, 2007).

Johnson, Lesley, 'Imagining Communities: Medieval and Modern', in *Concepts of National Identity in the Middle Ages*, ed. Simon Forde, Lesley Johnson and Alan V. Murray (Leeds: Maney, 1995), 1–19.

Makowski, Elizabeth M., *English Nuns and the Law in the Middle Ages: Cloistered Nuns and their Lawyers*, 1293–1540 (Woodbridge: Boydell, 2012).

Ormrod, W. Mark, 'The Origins of Tunnage and Poundage: Parliament and the Estate of Merchants in the Fourteenth Century', *Parliamentary History* 28 (2009): 209–27.

Ormrod, W. Mark, Bart Lambert and Jonathan Mackman, *Immigrant England, 1300–1550* (Manchester: Manchester University Press, 2019).

Page, William, ed., *Victoria County History of Buckinghamshire*, I (London: Victoria County History, 1969).

Smith, J. Beverley, *Llywelyn ap Gruffudd, Prince of Wales*, new edn (Cardiff: University of Wales Press, 2014).

Spear, Valerie, 'A Canterbury Lament', *Parergon* 18 (2001): 15–36.

Sutton, Anne F., 'Two Dozen and More Silkwomen of Fifteenth-Century London', *The Ricardian* 16 (2006): 46–58.

CHAPTER 6

Women's Issues in Parliament: Dower

Abstract Dower is the most common issue raised in petitions in Parliament by women (either in their own right, or in conjunction with husbands) during the later Middle Ages. Custom and common law upheld the right of the widow to one-third of her husband's landed possessions after his death. A significant proportion of petitions made in Parliament on the subject of dower complained about the thwarting of widows' rights by third parties and/or royal officials. The chapter focuses on petitions concerning dower made as a result of a series of turbulent political events between 1321 and 1330, when a significant number of women of noble and gentry status found their dower rights overridden as a result of the forfeiture of their husbands' estates for treason. Women claimed that, since they were innocent of rebellion against the Crown, they should be entitled to their dower. The Crown's response in 1327, as later in *c.* 1383 and 1399, was circumspect. But the way in which women pressed persistently for the principle that the widow ought not to be implicated in the offences of her deceased husband suggests that women were active participants in the process of parliamentary lobbying during the later Middle Ages.

Keywords Dower • Gender • Pardon • Parliament • Rebellion • Treason

W. M. Ormrod, *Women and Parliament in Later Medieval England*, The New Middle Ages,
https://doi.org/10.1007/978-3-030-45220-9_6

The Law of Dower

Medieval custom and common law upheld the right of a married woman, if suitably endowed by her father and guaranteed by her husband at the time of her wedding, to have a third of her husband's landed estate held in free tenure at the time of his death, and to hold it until her own demise, at which time it should revert to the deceased husband's heir (whether her own child or another relative).[1] An important feature of the law of dower was that the widow retained possession of the portion of her deceased husband's estate even if she remarried. This meant that widows were often more attractive as prospective wives than were maidens, for they could bring about an instant and substantial increase in the landed interest of their second (and subsequent) husbands.[2]

Widows were provided, under both common and statute law, with various means whereby they could seek satisfaction in the courts against heirs who refused to deliver them the due portions of their deceased husband's estates and against tenants who occupied the relevant lands without rendering them up to the widow.[3] There were, however, certain restrictions upon what the widow could do with her dower lands. First, she was forbidden from wasting such estates, in order that the asset should not depreciate in value during her period of tenure. Secondly, although she might alienate or lease property while it was in her possession, her husband's heir had the right to recover such lands following her death under the provision of the Statute of Gloucester (1278); two common petitions of the later part of Edward II's reign suggest that heirs not infrequently struggled to assert their rights in this respect.[4] Finally, the heirs of landholders could sue the widows of the deceased holders if these women took property beyond their entitlement.[5] The difficulties faced by families that had one or more long-lived dowagers controlling a substantial portion of the patrimony made for a good deal of dispute over the competing rights of widows and heirs. The intractable nature of a proportion of those and other related disputes also drove the parties to seek resolution outside the common law, by direct supplication to the king.

Parliamentary Petitions on Dower

As a result, dower was an extremely common issue in petitions presented in Parliament, especially during the late thirteenth and first half of the fourteenth centuries. Because the common law provided solutions to disputes on dower, and because Parliament did not countenance matters that could be remedied in the common law courts, the parties to a dispute over dower could not use Parliament as a place to instigate proceedings. Consequently, the extant private petitions presented in Parliament that concern dower were all brought because something had gone wrong with the common law process and the plaintiffs or defendants required royal intervention to remedy the matter. This makes all the more remarkable the total of extant dower cases brought in Parliament. Within the 'Parliamentary Petitions' section of the Ancient Petitions, there are at least eighty-one separate cases concerning disputes over dower.[6] The great majority of these—some sixty-four cases—were brought by widows acting as *femmes soles*. In a further ten cases, the petition was made in the joint names of the relevant widow and her new husband, who claimed the relevant dower as part of their joint assets. Only in a very small number of cases did men petition alone on the subject of dower.[7] This suggests that male heirs, and widows who remarried, had fewer problems than did single-status widows over the legal details of dower, and/or were more successful in securing their rights regarding dower through litigation in the common law courts. A body of common law writs and statutory legislation beginning under Henry II, extended by Magna Carta (1215 and subsequent re-issues) and amplified by the Statute of Westminster II (1285) had the general effect of making the Crown the champion of widows prevented from accessing their dower, and the large number of petitions on this matter presented in Parliament by widows suggests that women and their legal advisers were well aware of the immediate access to royal grace implied by this mechanism.[8]

A review of the eighty-one petitions on the subject of dower reveals a number of common issues. In respect of lands held in chief of the Crown, royal officials could sometimes deprive the widow of her entitlement to delivery of her full dower. In 1423, for example, Elizabeth, widow of Sir Henry Beaumont, complained that certain lands that made up part of her dower had been withheld from her by the royal escheators (the county-level administrators of the king's feudal rights) during the minority of the heir to the main estate, John Beaumont.[9] And in 1433, Margaret Darcy petitioned in Parliament to the effect that her dower lands in Ireland had been taken into the king's hands on the false pretext that she was dead.[10] Widows showed some determination to see off competing demands on their dower. In 1290, Joan de Sarstone reminded the king that her complaint against the withholding of dower by the constable of Dover, Stephen de Penchester, had already been heard (in the absence of both parties) 'in your chamber before your main Council' (*en vostre chanbre devant vostre chef conseyl*) at the Christmas Parliament of 1289; in spite of an agreement that Stephen would relinquish control of the estate on the production of written evidence of Joan's former marriage and her obtaining of a suitable document from the bishop of Winchester, Joan was still without satisfaction.[11] And in 1320, Eleanor de Seagrave petitioned in Parliament for delivery of her dower, based on property in Billingsgate, London; her due possession had been confounded, first by the general confiscation of all her deceased husband's property for debts owed to the Crown, and subsequently by a false law suit brought by other parties demanding ownership of the property.[12]

The fact that the Crown was entitled to confiscate the dower of widows of tenants in chief who remarried without royal consent was also a source of trouble. In *c.* 1318, Joan de Lacy (née FitzMartin, d. 1322), dowager countess of Lincoln, complained in Parliament that the dower allotted to her by her second husband, Nicholas Audley (who had died in 1316), had been confiscated because the marriage had not been sanctioned by the king; in spite of the fact that the Crown had agreed to restore the relevant lands to Joan and a whole series of writs had been issued on the matter, the keeper of the lands, John Giffard, was still refusing to give them up.[13] This issue also affected women holding in jointure with their husbands. Jointure was a form of tenure that placed the husband and wife as joint holders of certain lands; after the husband's death, the relevant property remained in the hands of the widow, who (unlike the case of dower) could manage it as she deemed fit, including alienating it to other parties. In 1354, the parliamentary Commons complained about the habit of escheators of seizing land held in jointure as a penalty for the re-marriage of widows without royal consent.[14] Under Richard II one particularly vocal widow, Joan Felton (whom we also encountered in Chap. 3), submitted at least three petitions in Parliament arguing that lands held by her in jointure ought not to have been seized by the Crown in recompense for debts owed to it by her late husband, Sir Thomas (d. 1381).[15] Joan's case was a strong one, since it was generally upheld that widows were not liable for the debts of their late husbands on lands held either in dower or by jointure.

The Consequences of Rebellion

The most interesting feature of women's petitions on dower submitted in the medieval English Parliament relates to the consequences of the long series of violent political changes that took place between 1321 and 1330. The general effect of this cluster of events was the seizure, at various points between 1322 and 1330, of all the assets not just of the leaders of rebellion against the Crown but also of their numerous followers among the baronage and gentry. Those of this number who were killed in battle, put to death for treason or felony, or died of natural causes also left a significant number of widows whose rights to dower were sometimes overridden by the Crown's desire to maximise its revenues from confiscated estates.[16] The notorious ways in which Edward II's favourites, the two Hugh Despensers, father and son, victimised some of the greatest heiresses of their generation, including Alice (née de Lacy, d. 1348), widow of Thomas of Lancaster, and Elizabeth (née de Burgh) the lady of Clare (d. 1360), are well known. Lady Clare's first-person account in 1326 of how she had 'sued at all the Parliaments these three years by bill asking the king's grace and redress of the above-stated wrongs, but could have no remedy or reply or have my bill[s] endorsed' speaks dramatically to the way in which the Despenser regime of 1322–1326 blocked the routes to parliamentary resolution of major disputes over the political redistribution of noble and gentry estates.[17]

This is not to say that women of the aristocracy and gentry were silenced in the Parliaments of the mid-1320s. Other widows petitioned at the same time for the release of dower lands which had been confiscated among the possessions of various of the rebels of 1322, including Lancaster's principal ally, Humphrey Bohun, earl of Hereford, who died at Boroughbridge; Roger, Lord Clifford, and Bartholomew, Lord Badlesmere, both executed for treason after the same battle; Robert Holland, one of Lancaster's greatest protégés, who defected to the Crown in 1322 but was still subject to imprisonment and confiscation; Andrew Harclay, who was loyal to Edward II in 1322 but betrayed him to the Scots in 1323 and was then subjected to summary trial and execution for treason; and Roger Mortimer, who had also been imprisoned after Boroughbridge and escaped to France in 1323.[18]

Three successive petitions of Philippa de Bradbourne submitted in Parliament provide a good example of the way in which this series of events impacted on women's rights. In 1322, Philippa complained she was entitled to possession of the whole of her deceased husband Roger's estate for the duration of her life under the terms of a trust set up by her husband's heir, Henry Bradbourne, but had been deprived of the estate by the escheator of Derbyshire as a result of the defection of Henry to the cause of Thomas of Lancaster.[19] The resulting inquiry found in Philippa's favour and the lands were returned, thus upholding the principle (as yet only implicit) that property entailed through enfeoffments to use (that is, trusts that prevented the relevant estate to fall into the hands of the Crown during a minority in the relevant family) was not subject to forfeiture for treason.[20] In 1325, however, Philippa complained again that the lands in question had been taken back into the king's hands on a legal technicality.[21] In Edward III's first Parliament of 1327, Philippa submitted her third petition, this time stating that the confiscation reported in 1325 had been the work of the recently overthrown Despensers.[22] After a five-year struggle through a series of major political disruptions, Philippa's persistence finally paid off and she secured her tenure of the Bradbourne estate.[23]

The other petitions that widows submitted for release of their dower lands under the political circumstances of the 1320s had a rather less secure basis in law. They seem to have been predicated on two overlapping but distinct assumptions: first that the king had a general responsibility to deploy his grace so that all widows, along with their children, had the wherewithal to maintain an appropriate standing in society; and secondly, but much more controversially, that a widow ought not, by natural justice, to suffer for the rebellion of her husband. Thus, Segrede de Berlay, who claimed dower from a manor that had fallen to the Crown among Thomas of Lancaster's possessions in 1322, mentioned in her petition that the king had personally granted that she be allowed possession of the relevant lands.[24] Catherine le Beysyn demanded her dower from the estates forfeited from Roger Mortimer in 1322 'according to reason and the law of the land' (*solom reison et lei de la tere*).[25] And Joan de Burghfeld, whose husband died at Boroughbridge, in petitioning for access to her dower rights, stated that she had never committed any kind of crime against the king and that, without her dower, she had nothing on which to live.[26] That female petitioners and their legal advisers raised such points suggests both a general expectation about the Crown's willingness to distinguish between right and wrong and a degree of unease on the part of plaintiffs at successive regimes' inclination to appease the widows (and thereby the heirs) of former rebels.

The keenness with which the political community at large regarded these various disruptions to the dower rights of widows was revealed forcefully at the first Parliament that followed the overthrow of Edward II and the Despensers, in 1327. The common petitions that survive from this assembly include a general request for the repeal of all unjust actions undertaken by the Despensers against Thomas of Lancaster and his followers, together with a guarantee of the rights of the heirs and widows of those dispossessed during the Despensers' ascendancy.[27] The new government acting in the name of the youthful Edward III responded to this with a general confirmation of Magna Carta, preferring to let matters take their course rather than to try to legislate in detail on all the wrongs that had been committed over the previous five years.[28]

The question as to whether widows had the right to claim dower in relation to lands forfeited from their husbands then came to a head in another common petition from the same Parliament:

> Item, the commonalty prays that women throughout the realm be dowered from the holdings that belonged to their husbands, even if their husbands are convicted and adjudged of felony, as they are married at the great expense of their kinsmen, and the right to dower accrues to them through their marriage.[29]

This petition exemplifies the viewpoint of the wife's family, who gave a dowry for her in the expectation that her husband would deploy it, and/or other lands and rights of his, to provide for her in widowhood. In political terms, it undoubtedly reflects the anxiety that had been unleashed by the confiscation of property from the king's enemies both in the aftermath of the civil war of 1321–1322 and, to a lesser extent, following the revolution of 1326–1327. As a point of law, however, it was unsustainable. Dower (as distinct from property held in jointure or enfeoffed to use) was not exempt from liability to the husband's forfeiture for felony or treason—although in the case of felonies, the forfeiture was only for a year and a day.[30] The formal reply to the 1327 common petition was therefore that 'because the request is contrary to the law, nothing is to be done' (*por ce qe la demande est contre la lei, rien soit fait*).[31]

By stating this point in such stark terms, the Crown made it clear that women seeking access to property confiscated from husbands who were rebels against the king could not take proceedings in the common law courts, and had to rely purely on the discretion of the current monarch, who might choose to mitigate the hardships suffered by such widows by making individual concessions to them as a matter of grace. The treatment of the Mortimer women provides a case in point about the arbitrary nature of royal decision-making on this subject. Margaret Mortimer (née Fiennes), the mother of the disgraced and executed earl of March, was put in custody, and her lands remained in the Crown's possession until her death in 1334.[32] By contrast, Edward III decided, 'at her request', to restore Roger Mortimer's widow, Joan (née Geneville) to the considerable swathe of lands she had inherited in her own right from her father, including the valuable lordship of Trim in Ireland.[33] The treatment of the family of Edward III's uncle, Edmund, earl of Kent also exemplifies the way in which royal favour could act to the benefit of aristocratic widows. At the Parliament of November 1330 in which Mortimer was condemned to death, Edward III accepted and acted on the petition of his aunt, Margaret (née Wake), the countess of Kent, for the restoration of her dower following the execution of her husband by the Mortimer regime earlier that year.[34]

The act of grace that led to the re-establishment of the dowagers Joan Mortimer and Margaret of Kent had implications, in turn, for Eleanor, widow of Herbert FitzJohn, who, since the latter's death in 1321, had faced numerous difficulties in effecting her rightful dower.[35] Early in Edward III's reign Eleanor had submitted a series of petitions in Parliament relating to lands that ought, she claimed, to form part of her dower but from which she had been ousted as a result of the apportioning of the relevant manors variously to Robert Sapy, one of Edward II's most conspicuous household knights, to Hugh Despenser the younger, and to Edward III's great friend, William Montagu.[36] In 1331, Eleanor recalled how she had sued in Parliament in 1327 for the recovery of her portion of the manor of Barnsley (Gloucestershire); Edward III had granted the manor to the earl of Kent, against whom she had sued a writ of dower; but this had been quashed by the forfeiture of Kent in 1330. Eleanor, who pointed out that she had now been deprived of her dower in Barnsley for more than eight years, was simply told that, since Kent's son had now been restored to his father's title, she would need to bring a fresh writ of dower against him.[37]

The re-apportioning of, and disputed claims over, rights of dower during the turbulent politics of the period 1322–1330 had therefore forced a significant number of women to petition in Parliament as the venue that they and their legal advisers perceived as most likely to understand their various plights and provide access to the royal discretion that they needed to have exercised in their cases. Under both Edward II and Edward III, however, the Crown was much more circumspect, directing many such petitioners back to common law remedies and, in 1327, categorically rebutting the argument that the wives of those men suffering the penalties of felony should nonetheless have free access to their dower. Behind this cautious approach lay an understanding among royal advisers that where common law remedies were available they ought not to be overruled by otherwise arbitrary judgments in Council and Parliament, and that the feudal rights of the Crown, which were an important element in royal patronage, had in turn to be carefully protected.

As a result, widows continued to have to assert themselves through petitioning in Parliament (and, increasingly from the later fourteenth century, before the prerogative courts) in the struggle to uphold their rights to dower. In 1348, Joan Peshale petitioned the king and Council in Parliament that she be allowed dower on the lands of her late husband, Adam, a prominent member of the Staffordshire gentry, and which had been confiscated by the Crown on the grounds that Adam was a notorious malefactor who had died in a state of rebellion against the king. In this instance, the petitioner's argument was not about her own innocence but concerned the fact that Adam had never been formally subject to prosecution for felony and that his property ought therefore to revert to his son, Richard.[38] Women might also petition for release from their own offences in relation to the claims of dower: in 1332 Maud de Pikeryng sued successfully for pardon of a trespass in claiming dower on lands held in chief of the Crown without a royal licence to do so.[39]

The general debate on the dower rights of rebels' widows bubbled up again in the aftermath of the Peasants' Revolt of 1381. The Commons in or after the Parliament of October 1383 complained that the relatives of those who had been put to death during the uprising without any judicial proceedings and whose names had not been included in the list of those excluded from the general pardon granted after the revolt were now claiming their rights to the deceased persons' property; in order to confound such demands, they requested that this category of rebel be formally declared as felons. The common petition specified four instances of such rebels and the counties in which the relevant possessions lay: Walter (or Wat) Tyler in Kent, Jack Straw in Essex, John Hanchach in Cambridgeshire and Robert Phippe in Huntingdonshire.[40] John Hanchach of Shudy Camps (Cambridgeshire) was a substantial freeholder with some aspirations to gentry status; he had been put to death on the orders of Henry

Despenser, bishop of Norwich for his part in a local uprising in 1381.[41] Intriguingly, a petition from Hanchach's widow, Anne, survives among the 'Parliamentary Petitions', requesting her rights in dower of the lands of her husband taken into the king's hands.[42] It is more than likely that Anne's petition was the prime example of the process to which the Commons took offence in *c.* 1383; the Crown's decision to approve the common petition and declare that all those put to death during the insurrection were to be considered convicted felons shows where official sympathy lay. And the absence of any response to Anne's own request indicates that, once again, the Crown had resisted any individual or collective concessions to widows left destitute as a result of the rebellion of their husbands.

The finale to this drama over the rights of the widows of rebels and traitors came in the first Parliament of Henry IV, in 1399. Among the series of calls that the Commons then made for the undoing of some of Richard II's arbitrary acts against members of the nobility was a petition on widows:

> Also, that it should be ordained that the widows of men who are forejudged or attainted of treason or felony should be endowed with the lands and tenements which belonged to their said husbands, in cases where the said wives were not guilty of the aforesaid treasons.[43]

The Crown's succinct response, that the common law should continue to obtain, effectively repeated the position that Edward III's government had adopted in 1327. There is, however, no rush of petitions from the widows of those declared traitors under Richard II and Henry IV in the same way as had happened in the last years of Edward II. The reason is that the number and social range of those affected by acts of treason under Richard II was much smaller and narrower than it had been seventy years earlier and that the Crown had already made out-of-court settlements with at least some the noblewomen widowed by the treason trials of 1397–1398, either by releasing their dower or by making compensatory maintenance allowances.[44] The most pressing case left over from the previous regime at the time of the first Parliament of Henry IV was that of Philippa (née de Coucy, d. 1411), widow of Robert de Vere, duke of Ireland and first cousin to the king. Robert had been put to trial for treason in 1388 and died in 1392. Richard II had allowed Philippa's right to dower in 1398, but nothing had been done to effect a transfer of property, and the revival of the act of attainder against de Vere by Henry IV in 1399 meant that her route to sustenance was blocked again. The Commons in the Revolution Parliament of 1399 specifically referred to Philippa's case in a petition separate from that given above, and the king made an expression of good faith, though it took another petition, this one in the Parliament of 1401, to shift him into action in favour of the duchess.[45] In 1404, Henry IV also responded positively to the petition of his cousin Constance of York, whose late husband Thomas, Lord Despenser had died at the hands of a mob as a result of his participation in the Epiphany Rising in 1400. Constance expressly requested that she be absolved of the stain of her husband's rebellion by requesting her own restoration to the common law in order that she could sue for her dower on the Despenser estates.[46] The general outturn of the common petition on dower in 1399 was therefore to uphold the principle that widows of traitors and felons had no automatic right to dower, but that the king's moral obligation to support widows in need meant that, at least at the top levels of society, he would generally use his discretion and grace to respond with generosity.

Conclusion

How, then, do we interpret the private and common petitions about dower presented in Parliament in the fourteenth and fifteenth centuries? In 2001, Paul Brand challenged the prevailing view that the practice of dower exemplifies the established rights of women in the landed classes during the later Middle Ages. He argued that cases in the common law courts at the end of the thirteenth century reveal a general and deliberate attempt to limit dower to those women who had 'earned' it by being old enough to have sexual intercourse with their former husbands and who had remained properly chaste within marriage.[47] More recently, Michael Hicks has also demonstrated that the theory of dower was often modified in practice during the later Middle Ages, as the relatives of the male and female parties to a marriage vied, competed and compromised over what might form the widow's portion of the husband's former estate.[48] The petitions surveyed here suggest that, in the face of competing claims, widows were highly aware of the possible advantage to be had from the direct access to royal grace that was allowed during sessions of Parliament. Clearly, they were by no means always successful. In some cases, they were directed back to sue in the common law courts; in others, their claims for compassion were carefully weighed against the Crown's preference to dispose freely of its feudal rights. In 1327, *c.* 1383 and 1399, the king and

Council in Parliament powerfully articulated their resistance to automatic claims of dower on the lands of felons and rebels. Accordingly, during the Wars of the Roses in the fifteenth century, the widows of defeated rebels depended, again, on the discretionary powers of the Crown in reversing acts of attainder against their husbands and thus releasing to them the lands they claimed as dower.[49]

On the other hand, the rush of petitions by the widows of those who had opposed the king in the civil war of 1321–1322 and the perceived campaign of the widows of the rebels of 1381 also suggests that women of the landed classes, properly advised by legal counsel, consciously pushed at established custom and statute on the law of dower in order to secure what they regarded as a point of natural justice: that wives should not be implicated in acts of felony or treason committed by their husbands. The royal resistance to such an argument in 1327 and *c.* 1383 arose not because kings were reluctant to treat individual cases with clemency, but because conceding the point on the matter of dower would simply open up a huge range of issues around the disposal of the felon's (or traitor's) assets, in which not only the Crown but also the immediate lord of the given offender had a direct interest. With the benefit of hindsight at least, we can see that those women who appealed to the king in Parliament as a matter of conscience with regard to dower rights on estates of the rebels of the 1320s were helping to pave the way for the notion, which became properly embedded later in the century, that lands held in jointure and enfeoffed to use were not normally subject to forfeiture for treason.[50] While the Crown's refusal to allow the principle that the dower should be returned to the widow of a traitor allowed it to uphold its feudal rights, it may also have helped precipitate the general move away from widows' reliance on dower and towards the establishment of jointures that endured for the life of the surviving partner in a marriage.[51] In such ways, we can indeed tentatively assert the influence of women upon and among the law-makers of fourteenth-century England.

Notes

1. For what follows, see Loengard, '"Of the Gift of her Husband"'; Loengard, 'What Did Magna Carta Mean to Widows?'; Loengard, 'What is a Nice (Thirteenth-Century) English Woman Doing in the King's Courts?'; Dobrowolski, 'Women and their Dower'; Hudson, *Oxford History of the Laws of England*, 447–51, 786–804; and Hicks, 'Crossing Generations'.

Customary law could be more generous than feudal and common law, allowing from a half to the whole of the husband's lands to the use of his widow: Bennett, 'Widows in the Medieval English Countryside', 72. Widows could also, under certain terms, claim half the moveable property of their deceased husbands, and widows in London were especially privileged in their dower rights: Hanawalt, 'The Widow's Mite'.

2. Archer, 'Rich Old Ladies'; and Friedrichs, 'Remarriage of Elite Widows'.
3. Walker, 'Litigation as Personal Quest'; and Walker, '"Litigant Agency"'.
4. *SR*, I, 46; and Ormrod, Killick and Bradford, eds, *Early Common Petitions*, 209–10, 212.
5. *SR*, I, 48, 75.
6. This total excludes the petitions made by queens in relation to their dower lands, analysed above, 29–30.
7. In one case, a man petitioned on behalf of his destitute daughter for the provision of dower from her deceased husband's estate: SC 8/60/2999.
8. For the development of writs in the twelfth century intended to protect the rights of the widow, see Biancalana, 'For Want of Justice', 518–33.
9. SC 8/92/4558, with resulting action in *CCR, 1422–9*, 99.
10. SC 8/105/5219, dated by Connolly, ed., 'Irish Material in the Class of Ancient Petitions', 36.
11. SC 8/197/9826, dated, transcribed and translated in *PROME*, I, 292, 350, 396.
12. SC 8/3/145, printed from the original in *RP*, I, 376–7.
13. SC 8/64/3159, with context provided by *CFR, 1307–19*, 170, 172; and *CCR, 1313–18*, 390. For an earlier petition from Joan on the Audley dower, see SC 8/167/8333.
14. C 65/18, m. 2, printed in *RP*, II, 260, and in *PROME*, V, 107–8.
15. SC 8/85/4215; SC 8/111/5505; and SC 8/111/5517. At the same time, Joan and her husband's executors were negotiating around a large sum of money owed to Sir Thomas by Edward III and the Black Prince: SC 8/85/4215; SC 8/104/5168; and SC 8/111/5509. For the outcomes, see *CCR, 1381–5*, 30, 33; and *CPR, 1381–5*, 9, 221. For Joan Felton see also above, 46. Thomas and Joan were the parents of Mary Felton, discussed below, 98.
16. For the Crown's (and the Despensers') use of the contrariants' lands, see Fryde, *Tyranny and Fall of Edward II*, 69–118.
17. Holmes, 'Protest against the Despensers' (quotation and translation at 209, 211): 'siwy a toutes les parlementz ces trois ans par bille requerant la grace le roi et redrescement des tortz suisditz, on vnqes ne poey auoir remedie, response ne bille endosez.' None of the petitions submitted by Elizabeth de Burgh during this period before 1327 survive; ironically, one that does, from Alice Rokulf (*c.* 1322–1323), claims that Elizabeth had

unjustly deceived her of her own rights in the lordship of Gower: SC 8/109/5449, printed in Rees, ed., *Calendar of Ancient Petitions Relating to Wales*, 173. For de Burgh, see also Underhill, *For her Good Estate*; and for Alice de Lacy, see *inter alia*, Mitchell, *Portraits of Medieval Women*, 117–21; Seabourne, *Imprisoning Medieval Women*, 148–51.

18. Bohun: SC 8/120/5960 (petitioners: Thomas and Nicola Hindringham), resulting in *CIPM*, VI, no. 538. Clifford: SC 8/151/7520 (petitioners: Robert and Matilda de Welle). Badlesmere: SC 8/74/3658 (petitioner: Idonia de Sellynge), with context at *CIM*, II, nos 586, 782. Holland: SC 8/8/371, printed in *RP*, I, 424 (petitioners: William and Joan de Multon); and SC 8/161/8006 (petitioner: Alice de Holdene). Harclay: SC 8/149/7450 (petitioner: Isabel de Whynnon); and SC 8/173/8604 (petitioner: Ermeiard de Harclay). Mortimer: SC 8/8/367, printed in *RP*, I, 423 (petitioner: Catherine le Beysyn). For the impact of the forfeiture of other, lesser rebels on widows' dower, see SC 8/6/282, printed in *RP*, I, 405 (petitioner: Margery de Orliton); SC 8/36/1776 (petitioner: Joan de Bristmereston), with context at *CPR, 1321–4*, 358–9; SC 8/62/3088 (petitioner: Christiana de Monzpinzon), with context at *CCR, 1318–23*, 469; and SC 8/70/3482 (petitioner: Dionysia de la Ryvere). See also the case of Joan le Foun, widow of Lancaster's steward in the honor of Leicester, discussed by Harris, 'Taking Your Chances', 179.
19. SC 8/8/396, printed in *RP*, I, 437.
20. *CIM*, II, nos 576, 597; *CCR, 1318–23*, 625; Bean, *Decline of English Feudalism*, 138. In similar vein, Maud Holland, the widow of the rebel Robert Holland, argued that the lands confiscated from her husband had been held in jointure between them: SC 8/117/5806, resulting in the release ordered at *CFR, 1327–37*, p. 117.
21. SC 8/200/9988, printed from the original in *RP*, II, 437 and noted in *PROME*, III, 458.
22. SC 8/158/7879.
23. *CCR, 1327–30*, 54.
24. SC 8/91/4532; for the context, see *CIM*, II, nos 719, 854; and *CCR, 1323–7*, 28. Segrede's husband (who must have died in or shortly after 1322) had previously complained that Lancaster had forced him to give up the manor against his will: SC 8/92/4556, with attached documentation at SC 8/92/4557.
25. SC 8/8/367, printed in *RP*, I, 423.
26. SC 8/95/4719. For another petition for dower from lands confiscated in 1322 specifying that the widow had committed no crimes against the king, see SC 8/36/1776.
27. C 49/83, m. 1, printed in *RPHI*, 117–18, and in *PROME*, IV, 28.
28. C 65/1, m. 2d, printed in *RP*, II, 11, and in *PROME*, IV, 23.

29. C 49/83, m. 2, printed in *RPHI*, 121, and in *PROME*, IV, 31: 'Item, prie la commune: qe femmes parmye la terre soient dowes de tenementz queux furent a lours barons, tut soient lours barons attayntz de felonie et jugez, sicome eles sont mariez a grant costage de lours amys, et droit de douuer lour encrest parmye les esposayls.'
30. Kesselring, 'Coverture and Criminal Forfeiture', 193–5.
31. C 65/1, m. 2d, printed in *RP*, II, 11, and in *PROME*, IV, 23.
32. Margaret had been previously deprived of her estate between 1322 and 1326, though she had initially been restored to her property after the succession of Edward III in 1327. See Mitchell, 'Noble Widowhood', 174, 179. For Margaret's petitions relating to her dower rights, see SC 8/61/3028, summarised in Rees, ed., *Calendar of Ancient Petitions Relating to Wales*, 89–90; SC 8/62/3076; SC 8/63/3110; and SC 8/127/6346.
33. *CCR, 1330–3*, 99, 105, 110, 269, 489–90, 520. The unexpected death of Joan's son, Edmund, in December 1331 meant that Joan also became the holder, in wardship, of two-thirds of the lands accorded to her grandson, Roger (who was later restored to the earldom of March): *CFR, 1327–37*, 339. See also, more generally, Holmes, *Estates of the Higher Nobility*, 14.
34. C 65/2, m. 6, printed in *RP*, II, 55, and in *PROME*, IV, 109–11.
35. Herbert FitzJohn's inquisition *post mortem* was not held until 1327: *CIPM*, VII, no. 95. For the argument in 1327 that lands claimed by Eleanor in Wales had been granted to the Crown by her father-in-law, John FitzReynald, and her successful counter-claims in 1331, see SC 8/111/5535; SC 8/168/8386; SC 8/172/8578; *CIM*, II, nos 1034, 1252; *CCR, 1330–3*, 232; and Davies, *Lordship and Society*, 45.
36. Suit with Sapy: SC 8/54/2680. Sapy's counter-argument was that the land in question, in the manor of Leckhampstead (Berkshire), had been granted to him for a life term by Piers Gaveston and that since Gaveston's forfeiture in 1312 the reversion had belonged to the king. For Sapy and this dispute, see Hamilton, 'Reassessment', 52–3. Suit regarding land granted to Despenser: SC 8/111/5537, resulting in *CCR, 1327–30*, 331–2. Suit regarding land granted to Montagu: SC 8/257/12805, with action at *CCR, 1330–3*, 449.
37. SC 8/17/812, printed in *RP*, II, 409.
38. SC 8/172/8580, printed in *RP*, II, 192. For the background, see Gross, 'Adam Peshale', 190–6; and for an earlier petition from Joan on the same matter, see SC 8/239/11903, originally enclosed with C 81/319/18336.
39. SC 8/180/8971, resulting in *CPR, 1330–4*, 250.
40. SC 8/20/970, printed in *RP*, III, 175, and re-edited, with full analysis, in Ormrod, Killick and Bradford, eds, *Early Common Petitions*, 177–9. This common petition was not enrolled on the parliament roll.

41. Hilton, *Bond Men Made Free*, 141, 181, 215; Dobson, ed., *Peasants' Revolt*, 239.
42. SC 8/116/5754.
43. C 65/62, m. 5, printed in *RP*, III, 440, and in *PROME*, VIII, 64: 'Item qe ordeigne sit, qe les femmes, apres la mort lour barons qe sont forjuggez ou atteintz de tresoun ou felonye, qe soient endowez des terres et tenementz queux furent a lour ditz barons, la ou les ditz femmes ne fuerent en coupe de les tresons avantditz.'
44. Ross, 'Forfeiture for Treason' 574 n. 5.
45. C 65/62, m. 11, printed in *RP*, III, 432, and in *PROME*, VIII, 47–8; C 65/64, m. 10, printed in *RP*, III, 460, and in *PROME*, VIII, 112–13; and Ross, 'Forfeiture for Treason', 561 n. 3. The 1399 petition included the statement that the new king 'wanted to be a good lord to her, and to his other cousins' (… *vorroit ester bon seignour a luy, et a ses autres cousins* …). The settlement conveniently skirted over the issue of whether Robert de Vere had been granted a divorce from Philippa in order to marry one of Anne of Bohemia's ladies, Agnes Lancecrona.
46. SC 8/187/9329, transcribed (with the response) onto the parliament roll of January 1404 in C 65/66, m. 10, and printed from the latter in *RP*, III, 533, and in *PROME*, VIII, 252–3. For the background and Constance's subsequent betrayal of Henry IV, see Pugh, *Henry V and the Southampton Plot*, 78–9.
47. Brand, '"Deserving" and "Undeserving" Wives'.
48. Hicks, 'Crossing Generations'. See also Palmer, 'Contexts of Marriage'.
49. Rosenthal, 'Other Victims', 221–2.
50. Ross, 'Forfeiture for Treason', 560–75. For enfeoffment of jointures, see Hicks, 'Crossing Generations', 34.
51. McFarlane, *Nobility*, 61–82.

References

Unpublished Primary Sources

Kew, The National Archives of the United Kingdom

C 49 Chancery and Exchequer: King's Remembrancer: Parliamentary and Council Proceedings.

C 65 Chancery: Parliament Rolls.

C 81 Chancery: Warrants for the Great Seal, Series I.

SC 8 Special Collections: Ancient Petitions.

Published Primary Sources

Brand, Paul, Seymour Phillips, W. Mark Ormrod, Geoffrey Martin, Chris Given Wilson, Anne Curry and Rosemary Horrox, eds, *The Parliament Rolls of Medieval England*, 16 vols (Woodbridge: Boydell, 2005).

Calendar of the Close Rolls Preserved in the Public Record Office, Henry III-Henry VII, 61 vols (London: Her/His Majesty's Stationery Office, 1892–1963).

Calendar of the Fine Rolls Preserved in the Public Record Office, Edward I–Henry VII, 22 vols (London: His/Her Majesty's Stationery Office, 1911–1962).

Calendar of Inquisitions Miscellaneous, 1219–1485, 8 vols (London/Woodbridge: His/Her Majesty's Stationery Office/Boydell, 1916–2003).

Calendar of Inquisitions Post Mortem, Henry III-Henry V, 20 vols (London: His/Her Majesty's Stationery Office, 1904–1995).

Calendar of the Patent Rolls Preserved in the Public Record Office, Henry III–Henry VII, 54 vols (London: Her/His Majesty's Stationery Office, 1891–1916).

Connolly, Philomena, ed., 'Irish Material in the Class of Ancient Petitions (SC 8) in the Public Record Office, London', *Analecta Hibernica* 34 (1987): 1–106.

Dobson, R. B., ed., *The Peasants' Revolt of 1381*, 2nd edn (London: Macmillan, 1983).

Ormrod, W. Mark, Helen Killick and Phil Bradford, eds, *Early Common Petitions in the English Parliament, c. 1290–c. 1420*, Camden Society 5th ser. 52 (Cambridge, 2017).

Raithby, John, ed., *The Statutes of the Realm*, 11 vols (London: Record Commission, 1810–1828).

Rees, William, ed., *Calendar of Ancient Petitions Relating to Wales* (Cardiff: University of Wales Press, 1975).

Richardson, H. G., and G. O. Sayles, eds, *Rotuli Parliamentorum Anglie Hactenus Inediti*, Camden Society 3rd ser. 51 (London, 1935).

Strachey, J., ed., *Rotuli Parliamentorum*, 6 vols (London: Record Commission, 1767–1777).

Published Secondary Sources

Archer, Rowena E., 'Rich Old Ladies: The Problem of Medieval Dowagers', in *Property and Politics: Essays in Later Medieval History*, ed. A. J. Pollard (Gloucester: Sutton, 1984), 15–31.

Bean, J. M. W., *The Decline of English Feudalism, 1215–1540* (Manchester: Manchester University Press, 1968).

Bennett, Judith M., 'Widows in the Medieval English Countryside', in *Upon My Husband's Death: Widows in the Literature and Histories of Medieval Europe*, ed. Louise Mirrer (Ann Arbor: University of Michigan Press, 1992), 69–114.

Biancalana, Joseph, 'For Want of Justice: Legal Reforms of Henry II', *Columbia Law Review* 88 (1988): 433–536.

Brand, Paul, '"Deserving" and "Undeserving" Wives: Earning and Forfeiting Dower in Medieval England', *Journal of Legal History* 22 (2001): 1–20.

Davies, R. R., *Lordship and Society in the March of Wales, 1282–1400* (Oxford: Clarendon Press, 1978).

Dobrowolski, Paula, 'Women and their Dower in the Long Thirteenth Century, 1265–1329', in *Thirteenth Century England VI*, ed. Michael Prestwich, Richard H. Britnell and Robin Frame (Woodbridge: Boydell, 1997), 157–64.

Friedrichs, Rhoda L., 'The Remarriage of Elite Widows in the Later Middle Ages', *Florilegium* 23 (2006): 69–83.

Fryde, Natalie, *The Tyranny and Fall of Edward II* (Cambridge: Cambridge University Press, 1979).

Hanawalt, Barbara A., 'The Widow's Mite: Provisions for Medieval London Widows', in *Upon My Husband's Death: Widows in the Literature and Histories of Medieval Europe*, ed. Louise Mirrer (Ann Arbor: University of Michigan Press, 1992), 21–45.

Harris, Simon J., 'Taking Your Chances: Petitioning in the Last Years of Edward II and the First Years of Edward III', in *Medieval Petitions: Grace and Grievance*, ed. W. Mark Ormrod, Gwilym Dodd and Anthony Musson (York: York Medieval Press, 2009), 173–92.

Hicks, Michael, 'Crossing Generations: Dower, Jointure and Courtesy', in *The Fifteenth-Century Inquisitions* Post Mortem*: A Companion*, ed. Michael Hicks (Woodbridge: Boydell, 2012), 25–45.

Hilton, Rodney H., *Bond Men Made Free: Medieval Peasant Movements and the English Rising of 1381* (New York: Viking, 1973).

Holmes, George, A., *The Estates of the Higher Nobility in Fourteenth-Century England* (Cambridge: Cambridge University Press, 1957).

Holmes, George A., 'A Protest against the Despensers, 1326', *Speculum* 30 (1955): 207–12.

Hudson, John, *The Oxford History of the Laws of England, II: 871–1216* (Oxford: Oxford University Press, 2012).

Kesselring, Krista, 'Coverture and Criminal Forfeiture in English Law', in *Female Transgression in Early Modern Britain: Literary and Historical Explorations*, ed. Robert Hillman and Pauline Ruberry-Blanc (Farnham: Ashgate, 2014), 191–212.

Loengard, Janet Senderowitz, '"Of the Gift of her Husband": English Dower and its Consequences in the Year 1200', in *Women of the Medieval World: Essays in Honor of John H. Mundy*, ed. Julius Kirshner and Suzanne F. Wemple (Oxford: Basil Blackwell, 1985), 215–55.

Loengard, Janet Senderowitz, 'What Did Magna Mean to Widows?', in *Magna Carta and the England of King John*, ed. Janet Senderowitz Loengard (Woodbridge: Boydell, 2010), 134–50.

Loengard, Janet Senderowitz, 'What is a Nice (Thirteenth-Century) English Woman Doing in the King's Courts?', in *The Ties That Bind: Essays in Medieval British History in Honor of Barbara Hanawalt*, ed. Linda E. Mitchell, Katherine L. French and Douglas L. Biggs (Farnham: Ashgate, 2011), 55–70.

McFarlane, K. B., *The Nobility of Later Medieval England* (Oxford: Clarendon Press, 1973).

Mitchell, Linda E., 'Noble Widowhood in the Thirteenth Century: Three Generations of Mortimer Widows, 1246–1334', in *Upon My Husband's Death: Widows in the Literature and Histories of Medieval Europe*, ed. Louise Mirrer (Ann Arbor: University of Michigan Press, 1992), 169–90.

Mitchell, Linda E., *Portraits of Medieval Women: Family, Marriage and Politics in England, 1225–1350* (Basingstoke: Palgrave Macmillan, 2003).

Palmer, Robert C., 'Contexts of Marriage in Medieval England: Evidence from the King's Court *circa* 1300', *Speculum* 59 (1984): 42–67.

Pugh, T. B., *Henry V and the Southampton Plot of 1415* (Southampton: Sutton, 1988).

Rosenthal, Joel T., 'Other Victims: Peeresses as War Widows, 1450–1500', *History* 72 (1987): 213–30.

Ross, C. D., 'Forfeiture for Treason in the Reign of Richard II', *English Historical Review* 71 (1956): 560–75.

Seabourne, Gwen, *Imprisoning Medieval Women: The Non-Judicial Confinement and Abduction of Women in England, c. 1170–1509* (Farnham: Ashgate, 2011).

Underhill, Frances A., *For her Good Estate: The Life of Elizabeth de Burgh* (Basingstoke: Palgrave Macmillan, 1999).

Walker, Sue Sheridan, '"Litigant Agency" in Dower Pleas in the Royal Common Law Courts in Thirteenth- and Early Fourteenth-Century England', *Journal of Legal History* 24 (2003): 215–36.

Walker, Sue Sheridan, 'Litigation as Personal Quest: Suing for Dower in the Royal Courts, *circa* 1272–1350', in *Wife and Widow in Medieval England*, ed. Sue Sheridan Walker (Ann Arbor: University of Michigan Press, 1993), 81–108.

Unpublished Dissertations

Gross, A. J., 'Adam Peshale: A Study in the Gentry Society of Fourteenth-Century Staffordshire' (University of London PhD thesis, 1989).

CHAPTER 7

Women's Issues in Parliament: Rape

Abstract Rape or (in Latin) *raptus* consisted of a number of offences in the Middle Ages: it covered both sexual assault and simple abduction, in the latter case including those cases where the female victim colluded with her abductor. This chapter surveys some thirty-three extant petitions on the subject of rape found in The National Archives series SC 8 that were definitely or probably submitted in Parliament. There was a close link between rape cases and statutory reforms, as in the case of the petition of Sir Thomas West in 1382. Four reasons are adduced for suggesting that complaints and debates regarding the law on rape were more prevalent than the surviving number of private petitions suggests: that other petitions disguise cases by using different language to that associated with the crime of *raptus*; that petitions on rape lodged especially in the fifteenth century tended to concern women of high status, which provoked more general consideration of the offence; that Parliament was seen as the court in which women stood the best chance of having natural justice in such matters; and finally that common petitions on rape employed notably emotive language as part of their rhetorical strategy.

Keywords Abduction • Elopement • Emotion • Gender • Pardon • Parliament • Rape

W. M. Ormrod, *Women and Parliament in Later Medieval England*, The New Middle Ages,
https://doi.org/10.1007/978-3-030-45220-9_7

The Law of Rape

Of all the topics concerning women raised in late medieval English Parliament, the most intensively studied in modern times is that of rape.[1] An understandably emotive issue, the term 'rape' has nonetheless to be understood in its medieval context. The Latin term *raptus* was used in the later Middle Ages to define a wide range of offences. Originally in the thirteenth century the common law seems to have drawn some distinction between *raptus*, which involved a direct sexual violation of the victim, and the modern English term 'ravishment' (*ravissement* in Anglo-Norman French, but usually rendered in medieval Latin by the term *abductio*), which meant the forcible removal of the victim, often with the intent of constraining her into marriage, but without necessarily including sexual assault. The lesser register of the term 'ravishment' is demonstrated by its use in relation to male victims; since there was no law of male rape in the Middle Ages, the ravishment of a boy or young man was understood simply to mean abduction with the usual intent of controlling landed property held by or due to him.[2]

A further complicating factor is that, at least in a proportion of cases, the charge of *raptus* may have been fictional, used by plaintiffs to have cases of simple abduction (which was only a trespass, punished by a money penalty) upgraded to full-scale rape (and thus treated as a felony liable to sentence of death).[3] Adding further to confusion on the issue, the keynote legislation on rape, in the Statutes of Westminster I and II (1275 and 1285), effectively elided *raptus* and ravishment.[4] Even so, abduction remained technically separate in law until 1487, not least because it was an offence that applied to male as well as female victims; in that year, possibly in response to some recent cases of female abduction heard in the courts, it was upgraded from a trespass to become a fully-fledged felony.[5]

Throughout the later Middle Ages, prosecutions under the legislation of 1275 and 1285 therefore included cases of three kinds: genuine sexual assault; abduction; and clandestine elopement, where a maiden heiress or widowed dower-holder conspired with her abductor to be removed from the control of a father or other male relative.[6] It is by no means always obvious in the records of such cases as to which of these categories actually applied under the general charge of rape, though the fact that so many charges were brought by men rather than by women victims has created a general assumption that the concerns of the male establishment about unwarranted claims on the family property by abductors tended to prevail over any real concern for the plight of deflowered women or of those abducted against their will.[7]

The second and third of the scenarios on rape sketched out above created a particular difficulty for the law of property, since members of the female victim's family were powerless to challenge the transmission of estates to the abductor once she had given her own consent to marriage with him. In 1382, in response to a petition brought in Parliament by Sir Thomas West and taken up as a general point among the common petitions, the Crown agreed a new Statute of Rapes which aimed to address cases where the abducted woman had subsequently given consent to marriage: her male kin were now allowed to pursue the abductor in the courts in order to recover the relevant property.[8] Later, in 1453, legislation was also issued as a result of a petition brought by Henry Beaumont on the ravishment and forced marriage of his widowed mother, Joan, by which any legal obligations to which an unwilling woman had been forced to consent under duress from her abductor could be challenged and declared nullified.[9]

Parliamentary Petitions on Rape

Despite the intensity of interest in this subject and the identification of the petition of Sir Thomas West as the key driving force behind the Statute of Rapes of 1382, no study has previously attempted to draw systematically on the private petitions submitted in Parliament on the subjects of rape, ravishment and abduction in order to consider the level of concern that was demonstrated by victims, their families, and more generally by Members of Parliament.[10] I have identified some twenty-one cases in the 'Parliamentary Petitions' section of the Ancient Petitions that explicitly reference rape, ravishment and/or abduction of women, along with twelve further cases in later sections of the Ancient Petitions that are likely to have had a parliamentary provenance. This makes a total of thirty-three cases in all.[11] In ten of the instances, the female victim of rape or attempted rape/ravishment was the petitioner.[12] In one further case, a female petitioner complained of the abduction of her granddaughter.[13] There are also two petitions concerning the abduction of nuns.[14] In the other twenty-two cases, the petitioners were men: usually the husbands or other male relatives of a victim of rape/ravishment/abduction, but sometimes the appealed rapist/abductor making a special case for his innocence in the matter.[15]

Women—and men—petitioned in Parliament on the subject of rape not because they had an expectation of changing the law but because they felt that there were special circumstances in their own cases that made it impossible for common and statute law to be straightforwardly applied. As with dower, so with rape, the provision of statutory rights enforceable in the common law courts meant that all the petitions on the matter brought in Parliament arose from some error or failure in the lower courts. Not infrequently, this was to do with the untoward influence of the alleged rapist/abductor. In *c.* 1310, Margery de Treverbin (evidently a widow) petitioned that Thomas de Gevely, already once outlawed for the rape of her daughter, Sybil, had repeated the offence against the young woman at her lodgings in London. Margery had sued a second writ in the king's court, but Gevely had entered the service of Sir Henry Beaumont (d. 1340), one of Edward III's close confidants, and no-one had therefore been prepared to act on the writ and give Margery and Sybil the justice due.[16] Similarly, in *c.* 1338, Robert Martyn of Yeovilton (Somerset) complained that a number of public officers, including the under-sheriff of Wiltshire, had conspired to have him indicted in the royal courts in order to confound proceedings against one John de Croucheston for the ravishment of Martyn's wife, Margaret.[17] In both of these cases, the answers provided to the petitions insisted that the cases in hand should go back into the common law courts. Ironically, the petitioners then suffered the consequences of arbitrary royal intervention when Edward II and Edward III respectively offered pardons to the alleged offenders.[18]

A further problem faced by those who wished to pursue allegations of rape through Parliament arose from the Crown's need to observe the rights of church courts in matters concerning marriage. A striking case in this respect is found in the common petition registered in *c.* 1381 on behalf of Sir Geoffrey Worsley, which claimed that, while Geoffrey was detained as a prisoner of war in France, his servant Thomas Pulle had defiled (*defoilla*) Worsley's wife and persuaded her to divorce her husband and marry him; this had the effect of bringing to Pulle the very considerable inheritance that she enjoyed in her own right both as an heiress and as the widow of an earlier husband, Sir Edmund Hengrave.[19] Geoffrey's wife, unnamed in the common petition, was Mary Felton, who subsequently made her own, very different, account of these events in the ecclesiastical courts, arguing that it was Worsley himself who had instigated their divorce, on the grounds that Mary had previously undertaken a clandestine marriage with Sir Thomas Breton.[20] This case exemplifies the considerable ambiguities and confusions that arose over determining what did and did not constitute a valid contract of marriage in the later Middle Ages. It also exposes the very obvious motivations of acquisitive-minded men to bend those rules and (with or without forced coitus) to compel heiresses and widows into marrying them for their own material gain.[21]

The Frequency of Rape Cases in Parliament

It is tempting to suggest that the disinclination of the royal Council to encroach either on the common law or on canon law meant that petitioning on matters of rape to the highest authority in the land, via Parliament, came to be seen as a somewhat futile effort. In statistical terms, certainly, it seems that there was never a flood of rape cases into Parliament: the vast majority of such judicial processes must have remained in the common law courts, while in other instances victims' families either capitulated to the abductor's wishes or sought forms of rough justice by which to continue their disputes with the alleged offenders. It is significant in this respect that the 1382 Statute of Rapes seems to have resulted in few prosecutions in the courts, and was very little represented in Parliament: most of the petitions lodged by men on the subject of rape are datable before 1382, and of the others only two seem to come close to the particular circumstances raised as an issue by Sir Thomas West.[22] It might be pointed out that the number of cases where women petitioned in Parliament on the matter of rape was higher in proportion to those brought by men than was the case in the common law courts; this may well reflect Parliament's status as a place of special refuge for those, including women and the poor, who claimed that the common law could not protect them. Nevertheless, on the basis of the evidence thus far adduced, it would be difficult to argue in any sense that the king and Council in Parliament saw themselves as having any kind of special responsibility there on the subject of rape.

It is necessary, however, to register four quite significant caveats to that general point. First of all, the number of cases may have been larger than the sources now allow. There are other extant petitions made in Parliament during the later Middle Ages that refer to what look like attempted abductions, but which are couched not in those terms but as acts of trespass upon a woman's property and for which, in most cases, the petitioners simply sought special commissions of oyer and terminer or other discretionary interventions by the Crown. Thus, for example, in 1382 Lettice, the widow of Sir John Kirriel of Westerhanger (Kent), petitioned against

Sir John Cornewall, itemising a series of hair-raising attacks that he had launched against her and her people since 1378 with the clear intention of taking her forcibly as his wife and thus accessing her property held in dower.[23] Such attempted acts of forced marriage should be given more consideration alongside explicit accusations of rape and abduction in general discussions of the levels of reporting and prosecution of rape in medieval England.[24]

Secondly, we need to note that the comparatively small number of rape and abduction cases that were addressed in Parliament are noticeably skewed in favour of women whose high status was sufficient to warrant more general remark. It is likely that there was some reaction at least among the king's councillors but also perhaps more generally among the Lords sitting on the panels to try private petitions when Alice (née de Lacy), countess of Lincoln and Salisbury in her own right and widow of Thomas of Lancaster, petitioned in Parliament in 1335 about her ravishment by Hugh le Frene.[25] Alice had already been subject to an earlier abduction in 1317; by 1335, she was in her fifties and under a vow of chastity. In spite of Alice's high status, Edward III refused to take action against her second abductor, who was a prominent member of his court; and the whole episode may have contributed to the myth of Edward III's own 'rape' of a lady of high standing identified elusively as 'Alice, countess of Salisbury'.[26]

In the later fourteenth and fifteenth centuries it also became possible to create public debate about an individual complaint of rape through the practice of petitioning the Commons to have a private dispute taken up as a common petition. We have already noted that the private petitions of Sir Thomas West and Sir Henry Beaumont resulted in changes to the law of rape through the passing of parliamentary statutes. Generating sympathy for the victims of rape in the sense of non-consensual intercourse was a good way of prompting more general expressions of concern among the political community. This can be seen in relation to three rape cases involving high-status women during the mid-fifteenth century: Isabel, widow of John Boteler in 1437; Margaret, widow of Sir Thomas Malefaunt in 1439; and Joan, widow of Sir Henry Beaumont, in 1453.[27] Isabel Boteler and Margaret Malefaunt brought their own petitions on their cases, whereas that submitted on the rape of Joan Beaumont came jointly from her son and one of the rivals for her marriage, Charles Nowell. In each case, considerable detail was accumulated by the legal advisers responsible for drawing up the originating petitions to the Commons, not least (in the first two instances) in order to pinpoint the difficulties of pursuing rapists on cases committed in palatine and marcher jurisdictions (areas in the north of England and in Wales that came under the direct rule of their lords, and where the king's authority did not normally run). Isabel Boteler had appeared in person in October 1436 before the Council 'in the chamber of Parliament' (though no Parliament was in session at the time), and this may account for the fact that her petition submitted the following January appears in two forms, one more elaborate than the other in terms of the suggestions made for the apprehension of the alleged rapist, William Pulle.[28] The format of Henry Beaumont's petition about the rape of his widowed mother also strongly suggests active collaboration with the Commons and/or the clerks of Parliament in the way in which it concludes with a general recommendation for the new legislation that ensued. In other words, all three cases were prosecuted, and taken up, as highlighting matters of more general concern in the apprehension and punishment of rapists.

Thirdly, we may note that, as with dower, Parliament was seen as a place where natural justice ought to prevail in the treatment of particularly complicated causes. The Crown's apparent reluctance to become too involved in rape cases already entrenched in the common law and church courts did not necessarily mean a loss of confidence on the part of those who resorted to the process of petitioning in Parliament. The rigid requirements of the law certainly sometimes appear unfeeling to the modern eye. When, in 1320, Robert de Reppes complained in Parliament about the ravishment of his ten-year-old daughter, who had been placed in the safekeeping of a female recluse in Doncaster (West Riding of Yorkshire), the Crown's response was distinctly business-like: if the petitioner's daughter were to bring proceedings in her own right, she might be heard in the courts, but Robert himself would have to be content with pursuing her abductors for the theft of the goods he had deposited with her.[29] On other occasions, however, petitions on rape registered in Parliament could bring down the full force of immediate royal justice. Alice de Neville's petition, submitted at the Gloucester Parliament of 1378, concerning the abduction of her granddaughter, Margery Nerford, and the failure of Sir Robert Howard to produce Margery before the Council for deliberation of the case, led to proceedings taken by the Council in Parliament 'in the presence of the said lady [Alice] as well as the said Sir Robert' (*en la presence de dit dame come le dit monsire Robert*).[30] In 1406, Sir Robert de Layborne complained of the abduction of his ward, the nine-year-old Margaret de Sandford, who was the heiress of his wife, Margaret, and her forced marriage to the son of Thomas Warcop, the sheriff of Westmorland. Robert specifically requested that the malefactors be brought to account before the present Parliament or, if there was insufficient time during the session, the king's Council. The endorsement to the petition records the agreement of the parties to put their dispute to arbitration; if, however, they could not agree on an outcome by that route, then they were indeed to come before the Council which, acting on the authority of Parliament, would deliver judgment.[31] In such cases, then, the recourse to petitioning in Parliament attracted the immediate attention of the king's Council, serving to break a deadlock in the courts and provided the means to out-of-court settlements for the rival parties.

The fourth caveat that needs to be expressed in relation to the smallness of the number of private petitions on rape registered in Parliament concerns the emotive language used by the Commons when they took up private petitions on the matter and/or proposed changes to the law of rape and its enforcement. A recently identified common petition dating from *c.* 1305–*c.* 1331 expresses concern at the frequency of the offence of ravishment and the harm that the crime did to the 'souls and hearts' of those immediately affected (*damage des almys et de coers a les persoins*).[32] On several occasions in the late 1370s, concerns were expressed in Parliament about the prevalence of ravishment in the king's palatinate county of Cheshire, and in 1382 the text of the Statute of Rapes declared that ravishers were 'in these days offending more violently in every part of the realm, and much more than they were wont' (*violencius et plus solito hiis diebus quasi in omni parte regni predicti invalescentes*).[33] In 1384, Parliament suggested the annulment of the recent Statute of Rapes on the grounds that its application was 'too harsh and strict' (*trop dure et redde*); on this occasion, it was the Crown that took the moral high ground and insisted that the legislation remain in force.[34] The statute of 1453 was particularly graphic in its account of 'divers people of power' who abused 'ladies, gentlewomen, and other *femmes soles*' and, 'perceiving their great weakness and simplicity', took them by force or dissimulation into their own control.[35] In similar vein, Henry VII's legislation on abduction described the crime as 'to the greate displesire of God and contrarie to the king's lawes and [to the] dispargement of … women and utter hevynesse and discomforte of their frendes and to the evyll example of all other'.[36] There is nothing especially unusual about the general tendency to an elaboration of language in the statutes during the fifteenth century.[37]

Nevertheless, the degree to which the Commons and the Crown expressed abhorrence of the crime of sexual assault suggests an emotional reaction quite beyond the ordinary rhetoric of politics. This can be illustrated especially effectively with regard to parliamentary concern about the pardoning of rapists.

Pardons for Rapists

Parliamentary debates about pardons were a major preoccupation in the first half of the fourteenth century. The specific cause for concern was the Crown's practice of giving out pardons for the capital offence of homicide. Successive kings were criticised for making free with such pardons in return for promises of military service, and on a number of occasions—in 1278, 1311, 1328 and 1331—the Crown was persuaded to issue statutes limiting this abuse by restricting pardons to cases of excusable homicide, which generally meant killing in self-defence.[38] It was this statutory restriction that Isabel, widow of Richard de Cleterne, explicitly referred to when, at some point between 1338 and 1343, she petitioned in Parliament requesting that a group of named malefactors, who had abducted her from her own home until she was rescued by Sir Anthony Lucy, should be denied their request for pardon. Isabel (or the clerk she employed to write the document) added, for additional effect, that she was making her petition 'for the love of God and the salvation of the king's soul, and for the honour of women' (*pur l'amour de Dieu et salvacioun del alme le roi et pur honur de femmes*).[39] In 1348 the Commons took the same approach by petitioning that 'murders, capturing of people, robberies, homicides and ravishments of women and other felonies and crimes' (*murdres, emblers de gentz, roberies, homicidies et ravissementz des femmes et autres felonies et mesfaitz*) should not be pardoned except with the express assent of Parliament.[40]

Susanne Jenks has recently elucidated the way in which murder and rape became excluded from the list of felonies and trespasses for which individuals could sue a pardon after the introduction of general pardons in 1362 and 1377. She has also shown that a further statute on pardons in 1390 was instrumental in defining the types of homicide that could not be reprieved by a general pardon as the most heinous of killings: those that took place in secret, those that happened in the course of an ambush or assault, and those committed intentionally (whether premeditated or not). The effect of the exclusion of murder from general pardons was, then, to draw a clearer line between homicide in general and the more serious manifestations of killing as the collateral consequence of other felonious activities or in cold-blooded vengeance.[41] It is worth noting, in the present context, that the parliamentary Commons actually petitioned the Crown in 1433 that one John Carpenter, who had murdered his sixteen-year-old wife only a fortnight after their wedding, perhaps in the belief that she was pregnant by another man, should be judged a traitor. Their argument (presumably) was that, since the killing of a husband by his wife was a statutory offence of petty treason, 'suche horrible mourdurs' by husbands of wives ought also to be thus judged. The Crown skated round the issue by declaring this a matter of matrimonial law and therefore within the scope of the Church.[42] But the case shows very clearly that male political society had a general revulsion of unreasonable violence towards women.

Did the development of a hierarchy of seriousness in homicide have an effect, in turn, on attitudes to rape? Jenks believes that general pardons—which, after 1414 actually allowed the pardoning of murder and rape—had no dynamic effect on the way in which rape was perceived or prosecuted.[43] This, however, is to ignore a previously neglected case that survives in The National Archives series 'Chancery: Council and Parliament Proceedings' (C 49) and on the parliament roll of 1445. In it, the Commons took up the case of Isabel, wife of Roger Bakeler, who had been murdered by one John Bolton because she would not allow him to ravish her. Bolton had been apprehended for the crime, but had become an approver (that is, turned king's evidence) and acquired a general pardon that acquitted its holder of the crime of murder. In line with the tendency towards the graduation of penalties for different types of homicide, the Commons argued that the killing of a woman who was defending herself against attempted rape should be declared an act of (petty) treason. They also recommended that no charters of pardon should be granted for any sexual assault that led to the homicide of the female victim. As in the Carpenter case of 1433, the complexities of the law were such that the Crown refused to act, and no answer was provided to this common petition.[44] Nevertheless, continuing public concern about the fact that murderers and rapists were covered by the general pardons periodically offered by the Crown may well provide a context for the later decision to exclude these offences, along with the abduction of women against their will, from general pardons issued in and after 1485.[45]

Rape and Emotion

Critiques of the statutory law on rape as it developed across the late thirteenth to fifteenth centuries, especially when informed by feminist theory, tend to see the trajectory as a move away from direct concern for the defilement of the female victim and towards the preoccupations of men with the property rights of the family.[46] Not all feminist scholars have agreed with this perceived pattern: Emma Hawkes, for example, has pointed to the continued use of emotive language in pleas of rape as evidence that right-minded men had an instinctive, emotional repugnance of forced coitus.[47] The foregoing discussion of cases of rape and ravishment brought in Parliament in the fourteenth and fifteenth centuries suggests that, whenever they addressed the topic collectively, the Commons demonstrated their strong revulsion over sexual assault through the use of heightened language. In their petition on the Isabel Bakeler case, for example, the Commons dwelt on each stage of the rapist's attack: the victim's resistance; the removal of all her clothing; the cutting of her throat; and the repeated stabbings she suffered to her breast and side. They went on to list the items of clothing and other possessions that Isabel had upon her at the time of her death in order to validate the additional charge of robbery against the perpetrator. This, however, does not have to lead us to presume that the Commons saw Isabel merely as another chattel of her husband, let alone that the question of property was now deemed more serious than the charge of rape. The idea of a crime against God's laws that damaged the 'souls and hearts' of those concerned was notably explicit in some of the wider political discourse on rape, ravishment and abduction that came out of Parliament.

In this sense, parliamentary attitudes do indeed indicate that rape remained a women's issue, both in the sense of creating anxiety and distress for victims and potential victims and in the sense of creating a more general debate among the male Members of Parliament about what should be done to set in place effective deterrents to would-be rapists and abductors. Parliament may well have been misogynistic in its views: the fact that the Commons never avowed a petition from a woman on the subject of rape must surely tell us something about the ways in which the patriarchy saw the relative value of men's and women's testimony. On the other hand, the Commons' willingness in 1382 and 1453 to champion the individual cases of Sir Thomas West and Sir Henry Beaumont such as to provoke new statutory legislation from the Crown, and the remarkable (if unsuccessful) common petitions of 1433 and 1445 on raising the crime of the killing of women who resisted sexual assault to the level of treason, suggest that there was a real will in Parliament to present a morally upright view of the crime of rape and to have the law of the land apply with due harshness to those who deflowered the daughters, wives and widows of the king's loyal male subjects. That claims of rape and/or abduction sometimes disguised the complicity of the alleged female victim in plotting elopement with a lover is undoubtedly true, though it is extremely difficult to pinpoint instances where this can be said to be categorically the case.[48] It would be quite false, however, to assume that Parliament judged the matter of rape solely in terms of property and expressed concern only when, as in 1382, it wished to prevent treasure-hunters from acquiring a woman's inheritance or dower by forced or complicit abduction. In forcing the Crown's hand on the law of rape on a number of occasions, and in the more general concerns that it exhibited over rapists who killed their victims and/or escaped justice because of conflicts of jurisdiction, Parliament demonstrated a consistent approach to what it clearly felt was one of the most morally repugnant and heinous of crimes.

Conclusion

Abduction and rape were widespread issues in the Middle Ages, and the story of their discussion in Parliament is only one aspect of the topic. Literary scholars, for example, have been much occupied with such questions since 1873, when F. J. Furnivall discovered a reference to a release made by one Cecily Chaumpaigne for the poet Geoffrey Chaucer. In this document, Chaumpaigne formally withdrew, to Chaucer's benefit, 'all manner of actions such as they relate to my rape [*raptus*] or any other thing or cause' (*omnimodas acciones tam de raptu meo tam de aliqua alia re vel causa*).[49] Scholars of Chaucerian literature, and more generally of the romance tradition of writing and reading in the later Middle Ages, have found in literary texts an abundance of references to the phenomenon of *raptus* and its moral framework.[50] This work, driven in recent generations by the feminist approach to the Middle Ages, has in turn served to interrogate the ethics of rape as they applied both in the fourteenth century and today, in an attempt to find a meaningful way of discussing the Chaumpaigne case and others like it inside and outside the classroom.[51] This chapter has attempted to avoid any anachronistic assessment of the moral dimensions of *raptus* as revealed in the records of the medieval

English Parliament. To a surprising extent, however, the uncovering of debates on the issue has revealed the strong sense of revulsion that Parliament, as a collective, exhibited towards this and associated crimes. All of this can, of course, be dismissed as so much hypocrisy: it was easy enough, no doubt, for men who might themselves have committed private acts of abduction to rage publicly against *raptus* when the political mood required it. However, the degree of care that the Crown exhibited to its own responsibilities in this matter acted as a model of patriarchal responsibility to the female sex, and established a code of behaviour to which all those involved in the polity might be expected to adhere. The numerous accounts of *raptus*, both real and fictional, that come to us in fragmentary form from the Middle Ages all have their back stories and their own individual features, such as to make it very difficult to generalise about men's actions, and thoughts, on the subjects of abduction and rape. In this sense the records of Parliament, like those of other courts, provide only snapshots of brief moments in time. Rape teaches us not only how much we can construct about medieval morality, but also how little we actually know about the extent or limits of the crime among the politically active classes, let alone the population as a whole.

Notes

1. See, most recently and thoroughly, Seabourne, *Imprisoning Medieval Women*, 89–104; and Dunn, *Stolen Women*. Both these works provide access to the extensive secondary literature on rape.
2. For the use of the term 'ravishment' in relation to a male victim, see SC 8/169/8432, printed in *RP*, II, 14 (1328).
3. See the discussions by Musson, 'Crossing Boundaries', esp. 91; Seabourne, *Imprisoning Medieval Women*, 193–7; and Dunn, *Stolen Women*, 1–17.
4. *SR*, I, 29, 87; Post, 'Ravishment of Women'; and Seabourne, *Imprisoning Medieval Women*, 92–3.
5. *SR*, II, 512; Ives, '"Agaynst taking awaye of Women"'; and Cameron, 'Complaint and Reform'.
6. See the comments of Seabourne, *Imprisoning Medieval Women*, 193–7; and Dunn, *Stolen Women*, 14.
7. See further discussion below, 101–102.
8. SC 8/147/7347; C 65/39, m. 3, printed in *RP*, III, 139–40, and in *PROME*, VI, 296; *SR*, II, 27; and Post, 'Sir Thomas West'. Seabourne, *Imprisoning Medieval Women*, 97–8, notes that SC 8/143/7132 (abduction of wife of petitioner) and SC 8/146/7264 (abduction of daughter

and wife; husband and wife as joint petitioners) both date from shortly before the Statute of Rapes, but the issues raised by these petitions do not seem germane to the specifics of that legislation. A second petition by Sir Thomas West, in 1383, referencing the recent statute and requesting its application in his case against his daughter's abductor, certainly suggests that the courts had been slow to move on the point: SC 8/146/7252, printed in Post, 'Sir Thomas West', 27.

9. SC 8/28/1362; C 65/102, mm. 2-1, printed in *RP*, 269–71, and in *PROME*, XII, 316–20; and *SR*, II, 367–8.
10. Seabourne, *Imprisoning Medieval Women*, 129–43, uses material from the Ancient Petitions to argue the importance which victims and other interested parties placed on seeking redress on rape outside the confines of the common law, but does not consider this evidence in a specifically parliamentary context. Surprisingly, Dunn, who has made the most extensive study of the subject of abduction of women in the later Middle Ages, actually omits the material from the Ancient Petitions altogether, including petitions entered in Parliament only when they happen to have been taken up as common petitions and enrolled on the parliament roll: Dunn, *Stolen Women*, 204–30.
11. A further case that appears only on the parliament roll (that is, without an accompanying original in the Ancient Petitions) is that of the accusation of Theobald de Verdun for the abduction of Elizabeth de Burgh, lady of Clare (d. 1360) in 1316: SC 9/20, m. 3, printed in *RP*, I, 352–3, and in *PROME*, III, 208–9. It is unclear whether this process was actually brought by petition; as an anonymous publisher's reader pointed out, this case is especially complicated, partly because the abduction occurred in Ireland and partly because Verdun died soon after, leaving Elizabeth pregnant.
12. SC 8/24/1175–1176, printed in *RP*, IV, 164 (Margaret Scrope); SC 8/27/1305, enrolled on the parliament roll at C 65/94, m. 6, printed in *RP*, IV, 497, and in *PROME*, XI, 206–7 (Isabel Boteler); SC 8/27/1316, enrolled on the parliament roll at C 65/95, m. 10, printed in *RP*, V, 14–15, and in *PROME*, XI, 271–3 (Margaret Malefaunt); SC 8/39/1937, printed in Fraser, ed., *Northern Petitions*, 99–100 (Isabel Cleterne); SC 8/64/3163 (Alice de Lacy); SC 8/76/3756 (Margery de Treverbin); SC 8/196/9760 (Joan de Braddene); SC 8/199/9943 (Idonea le Furmager); SC 8/209/10426 (Eleanor de Parys); and SC 8/343/16152, printed in *RP*, II, 34 (Olive Snard).
13. SC 8/18/889, enrolled on the parliament roll with subsequent judicial process at C 65/33, m. 4, and printed from the latter in *RP*, III, 39–40, and in *PROME*, VI, 84–7.
14. SC 8/97/4804; and SC 8/117/5838.

15. SC 8/3/143, with Latin summary in *RP*, I, 376 (Hugh de Lincoln: wife); SC 8/12/596, printed from a later copy in *RP*, II, 176 (John FitzJohn: third party's widow); SC 8/23/1108 (Robert Laybourne: heiress of wife); SC 8/28/1362, resulting in the process recorded in C 65/102, mm. 2-1, and printed from the latter in *RP*, V, 269–70, and in *PROME*, XII, 316–20 (Henry Beaumont: mother); SC 8/41/2042 (Thomas de Dakenham: wife); SC 8/51/2520 (Elias de Hawile: wife); SC 8/60/2979A (Robert Martyn: wife); SC 8/80/3999 (Roger de Quenby: wife); SC 8/86/4252 (Thomas and Alice Porthaleyn: petition made jointly in names of the husband and raped wife); SC 8/87/4307 (Robert de Reppes: daughter); SC 8/97/4844 (John atte Chirche: challenging an appeal of rape); SC 8/118/5858 (Henry Ilcombe: challenging an appeal of rape); SC 8/143/7132 (Gilbert Tiler: wife); SC 8/146/7252 and SC 8/147/7347 (Sir Thomas West: daughter); SC 8/146/7264 (Stephen Worlyk: wife); SC 8/146/7282 (Sir Hugh Wrottesley: daughter); SC 8/162/8054, printed in Rees, ed., *Calendar of Ancient Petitions Relating to Wales*, 271–2 (John le Clerk: wife); SC 8/219/10931 (Thomas de la Penne: wife); SC 8/256/12792F (Richard de Seyton: wife); SC 8/259/12929 (George de Percy: wife); SC 8/277/13828 (Richard and Elizabeth FitzWilliam: wife's mother, a vowess); and SC 8/334/E1158 (Adam atte Sonde: wife). My calculations exclude petitions from men making direct requests for the king's grace in granting pardons of rapes, which were generally submitted and dealt with outside sessions of Parliament. For some examples, see SC 8/175/8710; SC 8/179/8926; SC 8/181/9042; SC 8/183/9106; SC 8/183/9135; SC 8/185/9213; SC 8/186/9288; and SC 8/332/15752.
16. SC 8/76/3756. For Beaumont's relationship with the king, see Ormrod, *Edward III*, 22–3, 33, 39–40, 55, 149–50, 164, 165.
17. SC 8/60/2979A.
18. *CPR, 1307–13*, 362; *CPR, 1338–40*, 58, and see also 352–3.
19. SC 8/103/5109, printed and analysed in Ormrod, Killick and Bradford, eds, *Early Common Petitions*, 183–5.
20. Makowski, 'Curious Case of Mary Felton'; and Lacey, 'Petitioners for Royal Pardon', 47–51.
21. On the law of marriage, see (among a very large literature) Donahue, *Law, Marriage, and Society*.
22. For the low rate of prosecution, see Hawkes, 'Preliminary Notes on Consent'. The two petitions in question are SC 8/23/1108 and SC 8/86/4252.
23. SC 8/55/2713, printed and discussed in Ormrod, 'Needy Knights and Wealthy Widows'.
24. For one such discussion, see Hanawalt, *Crime and Conflict*, 104–10.

25. SC 8/64/3163. Alice subsequently consented to the marriage: Cokayne, *Complete Peerage*, VII, 687.
26. Ormrod, *Edward III*, 145. For the myth, see also Gransden, 'Alleged Rape'.
27. Boteler: SC 8/27/1305, enrolled on the parliament roll at C 65/94, m. 6, printed in *RP*, IV, 497, and in *PROME*, XI, 206–7; and see John H. Fisher, Malcolm Richardson and Jane L. Fisher, eds, *An Anthology of Chancery English* (Knoxville: University of Tennessee Press, 1984), 244–5. Malefaunt: SC 8/27/1316, enrolled on the parliament roll at C 65/95, m. 10, printed in *RP*, V, 14–15, and in *PROME*, XI, 271–3. Beaumont: SC 8/28/1362; SC 8/28/1362, leading to the process recorded in C 65/102, mm. 2-1, and printed from the latter in *RP*, V, 269–70, and in *PROME*, XII, 316–20, and resulting in *CPR, 1452–61*, 60. For detailed discussion of the first two cases, see Sinclair, 'The "Ravishing" of Isabel Boteler'; Griffiths, 'Pursuit of Justice'. See also Dodd, 'Blood, Brains and Bay-Windows', 25–6.
28. E 28/58/60, discussed in *PROME*, XI, 199.
29. SC 8/87/4307. For the ways in which the courts dealt with cases of child rape, see Kissane, '"Unnatural in body"'. Kissane (96–7) also discusses and contextualises the case of the seven-year-old Idonea le Furmager (SC 8/199/9943).
30. SC 8/18/889, enrolled with a further account of proceedings in C 65/33, m. 4, and printed from the latter in *RP*, III, 39–40, and in *PROME*, VI, 84–7. For context, see *CCR, 1377–81*, 204, 220, 227–8; *CPR, 1377–81*, 307, 309, 311. For Margery, see Erler, *Women, Reading, and Piety*, 48–67.
31. SC 8/23/1108, printed from the original in *RP*, III, 564–5. This idea of Parliament as a potentially potent force in such matters is echoed tangentially in a petition of 1446 that references the abduction and forced marriage of Alice Porthaleyn at Highgate (Middlesex) and commented specifically on the brazen nature of the crime, committed within three miles of London while Parliament was in session: SC 8/86/4252.
32. SC 8/55/7740, printed and analysed in Ormrod, Killick and Bradford, eds, *Early Common Petitions*, 191–7, with the relevant clause and discussion at 193, 196.
33. C 65/33, m. 3, printed in *RP*, III, 42–3, and in *PROME*, VI, 91; C 65/34, m. 4, printed in *RP*, III, 62, and in *PROME*, VI, 124; and C 65/35, m. 4, printed in *RP*, III, 81, and in *PROME*, VI, 167–8; *SR*, II, 27.
34. C 65/42, m. 1, printed in *RP*, III, 174, and in *PROME*, VI, 379–80.
35. *SR*, II, 367–8: *divers gens de poiar ... dames et gentilx femmes et autres femmes esteantz soulz ... la graunte innocencie et simples de eux.*
36. *SR*, II, 512.
37. Dodd, 'Kingship, Parliament and the Court'.
38. Lacey, *Royal Pardon*, 22–3.

39. SC 8/39/1937, printed in Fraser, ed., *Northern Petitions*, 99–100.
40. C 65/13, m. 3, printed in *RP*, II, 172, and in *PROME*, IV, 430. Seabourne, *Imprisoning Medieval Women*, 97 suggests that this petition may have been prompted by the case of Margery de la Beche (*CPR, 1345–8*, 318), but there is nothing to suggest that ravishment was being dealt with separately from the other stated felonies.
41. Jenks, 'Exceptions in General Pardons', 157–62.
42. SC 8/26/1281, enrolled as C 65/92, m. 5, and printed from the latter source in *RP*, IV, 447, and in *PROME*, XI, 130–1.
43. Jenks, 'Exceptions in General Pardons', 162–3.
44. C 49/26/5, enrolled on the parliament roll as C 65/97, m. 4, and printed from the latter in RP, V, 111–12, in *PROME*, XI, 490–1, and in Fisher, Richardson and Fisher, eds, *Anthology of Chancery English*, 260–2. The only other discussion of the case of which I am aware is Dodd, 'Blood, Brains and Bay-Windows', 25.
45. *SR*, II, 504; Jenks, 'Exceptions in General Pardons', 158, 181.
46. Phillips, 'Written on the Body'.
47. Hawkes, '"She was ravished against her will"'.
48. For an extended analysis concluding that *raptus* emphatically involved forced coitus, see Christopher Cannon, '*Raptus* in the Chaumpaigne Release'. Contrarily, for another detailed study that emphasises the fictional nature of some claims of sexual assault and the consent of supposed female victims, see Kelly, 'Statutes of Rapes'. For further, more recent discussions of the various forms that *raptus* and ravishment could take in the later Middle Ages, see Goldberg, *Communal Discord*, 162–7; and Dunn, 'Prosecuting Ravishment'.
49. Crow and Olsen, eds, *Chaucer Life Records*, 344–5, cited by Cannon, '*Raptus* in the Chaumpaigne Release', 74.
50. Among book-length studies, see Saunders, *Rape and Ravishment*; and Edwards, *Afterlives of Rape*.
51. See, for example, Hanawalt, *'Of Good and Ill Repute'*, 124–41; Waymack, 'Teaching *de raptu meo*'.

References

Unpublished Primary Sources

Kew, The National Archives of the United Kingdom
C 49 Chancery and Exchequer: King's Remembrancer: Parliamentary and Council Proceedings.
C 65 Chancery: Parliament Rolls.

E 28 Exchequer: Treasury of Receipt: Council and Privy Seal Records.
SC 8 Special Collections: Ancient Petitions.
SC 9 Special Collections: Parliament Rolls, Exchequer Series.

Published Primary Sources

Brand, Paul, Seymour Phillips, W. Mark Ormrod, Geoffrey Martin, Chris Given Wilson, Anne Curry and Rosemary Horrox, eds, *The Parliament Rolls of Medieval England*, 16 vols (Woodbridge: Boydell, 2005).

Calendar of the Patent Rolls Preserved in the Public Record Office, Henry III–Henry VII, 54 vols (London: Her/His Majesty's Stationery Office, 1891–1916).

Crow, Martin M. and Clair C. Olsen, eds, *Chaucer Life Records* (Oxford: Clarendon Press, 1966).

Fisher, John H., Malcolm Richardson and Jane L. Fisher, eds, *An Anthology of Chancery English* (Knoxville: University of Tennessee Press, 1984).

Fraser, Constance M., ed., *Northern Petitions Illustrative of Life in Berwick, Cumbria and Durham in the Fourteenth Century*, Surtees Society 194 (Gateshead, 1981).

Ormrod, W. Mark, Helen Killick and Phil Bradford, eds, *Early Common Petitions in the English Parliament, c. 1290–c. 1420*, Camden Society 5th ser. 52 (Cambridge, 2017).

Raithby, John, ed., *The Statutes of the Realm*, 11 vols (London: Record Commission, 1810–1828).

Rees, William, ed., *Calendar of Ancient Petitions Relating to Wales* (Cardiff: University of Wales Press, 1975).

Strachey, J., ed., *Rotuli Parliamentorum*, 6 vols (London: Record Commission, 1767–1777).

Published Secondary Sources

Cameron, A., 'Complaint and Reform in Henry VII's Reign: The Origins of the Statute of 3 Henry VII, c. 2?', *Bulletin of the Institute of Historical Research* 51 (1978): 83–9.

Cannon, Christopher, '*Raptus* in the Chaumpaigne Release and a Newly Discovered Document Concerning the Life of Geoffrey Chaucer', *Speculum* 68 (1993): 74–94.

Dodd, Gwilym, 'Blood, Brains and Bay-Windows: The Use of English in Fifteenth-Century Parliamentary Petitions', in *Petitions and Strategies of Persuasion in the Middle Ages: The English Crown and the Church, c. 1200–c. 1500*, ed. Thomas W. Smith and Helen Killick (York: York Medieval Press, 2018), 11–39.

Dodd, Gwilym, 'Kingship, Parliament and the Court: The Emergence of "High Style" in Petitions to the English Crown, *c.* 1350–1405', *English Historical Review* 129 (2014): 515–48.

Donahue, Charles, *Law, Marriage, and Society in the Later Middle Ages* (Cambridge: Cambridge University Press, 2007).

Dunn, Caroline, 'Prosecuting Ravishment in Thirteenth-Century England', in *Thirteenth Century England XIII*, ed. Janet Burton, Frédérique Lachaud, Phillipp Schofield, Karen Stöber and Björn Weiler (Woodbridge: Boydell, 2011), 63–81.

Dunn, Caroline, *Stolen Women in Medieval England* (Cambridge: Cambridge University Press, 2013).

Edwards, Suzanne, *The Afterlives of Rape in Medieval English Literature* (Basingstoke: Palgrave Macmillan, 2016).

Erler, Mary C., *Women, Reading, and Piety in Late Medieval England* (Cambridge: Cambridge University Press, 2002).

Goldberg, Jeremy, *Communal Discord, Child Abduction, and Rape in the Later Middle Ages* (Basingstoke: Palgrave Macmillan, 2008).

Gransden, Antonia, 'The Alleged Rape by Edward III of the Countess of Salisbury', *English Historical Review* 87 (1972): 333–44.

Griffiths, Ralph A., 'The Pursuit of Justice and Inheritance from Marcher Lordships to Parliament: The Implications of Margaret Malefaunt's Abduction in Gower in 1438', in *The Fifteenth Century XIV: Essays Presented to Michael Hicks*, ed. Linda Clark (Woodbridge: Boydell, 2015), 77–90.

Hanawalt, Barbara A., *Crime and Conflict in English Communities, 1300–1348* (Cambridge, Massachusetts: Harvard University Press, 1979).

Hanawalt, Barbara A., *'Of Good and Ill Repute': Gender and Social Control in Medieval England* (Oxford: Oxford University Press, 1998).

Hawkes, Emma, 'Preliminary Notes on Consent in the 1382 Rape and Ravishment Laws of Richard II', *Legal History* 11 (2007): 117–32.

Hawkes, Emma, '"She was ravished against her will, what so ever she say": Female Consent to Rape and Ravishment in Late Medieval England', *Limina* 1 (1995): 47–54.

Ives, E. W., '"Agaynst taking awaye of Women": The Inception and Operation of the Abduction Act of 1487', in *Wealth and Power in Tudor England: Essays Presented to S. T. Bindoff*, ed. E. W. Ives, R. J. Knecht and J. J. Scarisbrick (London: Athlone Press, 1978), 21–45.

Jenks, Susanne, 'Exceptions in General Pardons, 1399–1450', in *The Fifteenth Century XIII. Exploring the Evidence: Commemoration, Administration and the Economy*, ed. Linda S. Clark (Woodbridge: Boydell, 2014), 153–81.

Kelly, Henry Ansgar, 'Statutes of Rapes and Alleged Ravishers: A Context for the Charges against Thomas Malory, Knight', *Viator* 28 (1997): 316–419.

Kissane, Alan, '"Unnatural in body and a villain in soul": Rape and Sexual Violence towards Girls under the Age of Canonical Consent in Late Medieval England', in *Fourteenth Century England X*, ed. Gwilym Dodd (Woodbridge: Boydell, 2018), 89–111.

Lacey, Helen, 'Petitioners for Royal Pardon in Fourteenth-Century England', in *Petitions and Strategies of Persuasion in the Middle Ages: The English Crown and the Church, c. 1200–c. 1500*, ed. Thomas W. Smith and Helen Killick (York: York Medieval Press, 2018), 40–63.

Lacey, Helen, *The Royal Pardon: Access to Mercy in Fourteenth-Century England* (York: York Medieval Press, 2009).

Makowski, Elizabeth M., 'The Curious Case of Mary Felton', in *Proceedings of the Fourteenth International Congress of Medieval Canon Law, Toronto, 5–11 August 2012*, ed. Joseph Goering, Stephen Dusil and Andreas Thier, Monumenta Iuris Canonici Series C: Subsidia 15 (Vatican City: Vatican Library, 2016), 733–41.

Musson, Anthony, 'Crossing Boundaries: Attitudes to Rape in Late Medieval England', in *The Boundaries of the Law: Geography, Gender and Jurisdiction in Medieval and Early Modern Europe*, ed. Anthony Musson (Aldershot: Ashgate, 2005), 84–101.

Ormrod, W. Mark, *Edward III* (London: Yale University Press, 2011).

Ormrod, W. Mark, 'Needy Knights and Wealthy Widows: The Encounters of John Cornewall and Lettice Kirriel, 1378–82', in *The Medieval Python: The Purposive and Provocative Work of Terry Jones*, ed. R. F. Yeager and Toshiyuki Takamiya (Basingstoke: Palgrave Macmillan, 2012), 137–50.

Phillips, Kim, 'Written on the Body: Reading Rape from the Twelfth to Fifteenth Centuries', in *Medieval Women and the Law*, ed. Noël James Menuge (Woodbridge: Boydell, 2000), 125–44.

Post, J. B., 'Ravishment of Women and the Statutes of Westminster', in Legal Records and the Historian, ed. J. H. Baker (London: Royal Historical Society, 1978), 150–64.

Post, J. B., 'Sir Thomas West and the Statute of Rapes, 1382', *Bulletin of the Institute of Historical Research* 53 (1980): 24–30.

Saunders, Corinne, *Rape and Ravishment in the Literature of Medieval England* (Woodbridge: Boydell, 2001).

Seabourne, Gwen, *Imprisoning Medieval Women: The Non-Judicial Confinement and Abduction of Women in England, c. 1170–1509* (Farnham: Ashgate, 2011).

Sinclair, Shelley A., 'The "Ravishing" of Isabel Boteler: Abduction and the Pursuit of Wealth in Lancastrian England', *The Ricardian* 11 (1997–1999): 546–57.

Waymack, Anna, 'Teaching *de raptu meo*: Chaucer, Champaigne, and Consent in the Classroom', *Medieval Feminist Forum: A Journal of Gender and Sexuality* 53 (2017): 150–75.

CHAPTER 8

Women, Parliament and the Public Sphere

Abstract Women as a social group were considered by Parliament in a number of instances during the later Middle Ages. The chapter surveys two issues where women were explicitly recognised as active players: in the world of work, and in the public finances. In spite of the fact that women were a more important element in the workforce after the Black Death, Parliament preserved and enshrined the accustomed distinction between men's (higher) wages and women's (lower) wages in the labour legislation of the fourteenth and fifteenth centuries. In terms of the public finances, women petitioned in Parliament on a range of issues, not least the difficulties they encountered as executrices of their deceased husbands in clearing the debts owed by the latter as collectors of taxes. Women also petitioned in Parliament for recovery of debts from the Crown. In particular, the confident manner in which Emmotte Esmond went about claiming money owed to her by Henry IV indicates that women could be persistent lobbyists in the late medieval Parliament.

Keywords Finance • Gender • Parliament • Taxation • Work

W. M. Ormrod, *Women and Parliament in Later Medieval England*, The New Middle Ages,
https://doi.org/10.1007/978-3-030-45220-9_8

Introduction

Chapters 6 and 7 analyse the two key areas of public political debate—dower and rape—in which the experience of woman was most obviously to the fore in later medieval England. Both topics are ones in which patriarchy was particularly evident: on the one hand, the anxiety of the son and other male members of the family about the widowed mother's legal right to a substantial part of the patrimony; and on the other, the potential loss of reputation, and thus of worth, that a father suffered if his daughter was deflowered in an act of abduction. In this chapter, we turn away from individual petitioners to the medieval Parliament and to the more general debates that went on in the parliamentary Commons about the state of the economy, the public finances, and proposed reforms of the law. The historian Joan Scott wrote in 1986 that high politics is deeply gendered, but only insofar that it serves to objectify women as excluded from its processes.[1] This, as we have seen, is an undeniable fact so far as the membership of Parliament (both Lords and Commons) is concerned. Yet the political activism of women as petitioners in the English Parliament during the later Middle Ages shows irrefutably that they were confident in the place allotted to them in the public business of the realm and could organise their cases in such a way as to encourage action and remedy. That women petitioned in Parliament on a regular basis helps to call into question the older 'exceptionalist' approach, which tended to view women's deployment of public power in the Middle Ages as highly individualised and thus running counter to what were deemed the appropriate political and social norms. As Heather J. Tanner, Laura L. Gathagan and Lois L. Huneycutt have recently stressed, scholarship of the last and present generations serves to undermine the public-private dichotomy in gender studies and highlights the need for new categories of analysis.[2] It is tempting to assume from the discussion in the previous two chapters that the rights of women were only discussed in Parliament when the subject matter reflected issues in which men had strong interests. But there were other fields of public life discussed in Parliament in which women were directly and explicitly involved alongside men, with or without a conscious sense of the particularities of their gender. The inclusion of women either as passive or as active participants in these areas of business helps us to acknowledge the ways in which Parliament understood the place of women in political life. We may briefly discuss two such public debates: the economics of work; and the public finances.

Women and Work

It is no surprise to discover that Parliament was deeply conservative in terms of the roles that it allowed women in the spheres of profession and employment. In 1421 an unenrolled common petition called for the general regulation of physicians with a view to restricting practice to those with formal university qualifications. The petition went so far as to call for a formal ban on women physicians within the realm.[3] The exclusion of women from this activity was already implicit in the idea of training in formal, male-only institutions; the number of women who have so far been identified as claiming knowledge as physicians in late medieval England remains extremely small.[4] This no doubt explains why the government did not even mention women in the formal ordinance on the matter recorded on the parliament roll in 1421.[5]

At lower levels in the economy, by contrast, Parliament was content, indeed insistent, that women should form part of the workforce. The programme of legislation rolled out over the century that followed the arrival of the plague specifically acknowledged the important part that women came to play in this period within the agricultural and manufacturing economies. The major question that arises is the degree to which Parliament actually valued women's work. The earliest legislation to deal with the sudden rise in demands for wages as a result of the scarcity of workers, the Ordinance and Statute of Labourers of 1349 and 1351, referred to female workers only in the sense that the new laws were said to apply to 'workers, both men and women' (*servantz, sibien homes comme femmes*).[6] Soon, however, the Commons and/or the king's Council were to realise the need for making explicit provision for women. When, on the prompting of the Commons in 1363, the Crown issued a statute requiring that skilled men practise only one craft, the Council inserted an additional clause stating that the new restriction would not apply to women working in brewing, in baking or in the processing of wool and cloth. This was a clear admission of the fact that women's work was often casual and therefore multi-faceted, and was often based in the domestic environment of the household rather than the masculine world of the workshop.[7]

From 1388, moreover, the labour laws began to differentiate between the rates of pay for men and women in the agricultural workforce: a 'woman labourer' (*femme laborer*) was to have a maximum annual wage of 6s., which was comparable to that offered for male swineherds and ploughmen, but significantly less than the 10s. that could be commanded by carters and shepherds—jobs which, it was assumed, were only done by men.[8] As time went on, the margins grew: by 1445, the carter or shepherd was allowed to draw up to £1 a year (a 100 per cent increase since 1388) plus clothing (valued at 4s.) and subsistence, whereas the 'woman worker' (*femme servaunt*) was now entitled only to a maximum of 10s. a year (a 67 per cent increase since 1388), plus the same perquisites.[9] The day rates now specified for harvest work set the same ceiling for both men and women; but from the late fourteenth century the labour legislation had also been emphatic that pay should reflect local circumstances. In this sense, we can see that Parliament was complicit with the laws of supply and demand, which determined that women, like old and infirm males, tended to receive lower wages than able-bodied men.[10] In the area of work, then, Parliament exhibited a clear institutional discrimination against the higher visibility that women had in the workforce during the era of the Black Death.

Women and the Public Finances

Parliament was a vital institution for the management of the public finances, since it was in assemblies of Parliament that the Crown negotiated direct and indirect taxes and discussed the loans that would often be taken out on the expectation of future tax income.[11] Women were participants in this fiscal system in the sense that *femmes soles* could be liable to taxation. Down to the early 1330s, women were assessed for direct taxes only if they were householders in their own right with moveable property valued above an agreed (and fluctuating) taxable minimum.[12] After a series of changes in the tax system in 1334, however, the taxable minimum was dropped and a wider range of lower-status single women, like their male counterparts, became theoretically liable to pay.[13] The logical conclusion to this process was reached in the poll taxes of 1377–1381, which extended the fiscal net still further to include almost all unmarried females over the age of fourteen, sixteen or fifteen (in 1377, 1379 and 1380 respectively); only the indigent poor were now declared exempt.[14] Comprehensive poll taxes were not employed again after the discrediting of these experiments in the Peasants' Revolt of 1381. But women continued to be caught in the tax net, either because (as before 1377) they held liable property under *femme sole* status or because single women were specified as liable to some of the experimental taxes of the fifteenth century, such as the income taxes on landed society and the special subsidies imposed on alien residents of the realm.[15]

The paying of taxes was often inevitably done begrudgingly, and was sometimes actively resisted; in this way, the involvement of women in some of the violent affrays that took place during the Peasants' Revolt of 1381 can be read as direct protests against their sudden inclusion into the public administration of royal finance.[16] But under the standard forms of direct taxation, liability could also be seen as an acknowledgement of householders' standing as fully invested members of their local communities, and of their general participation in public life.[17] Not that this position itself was without its trials. A widow of gentry status who served as executrix of her husband's will might find herself caught up for years wrangling with the Exchequer over his debts as a collector of taxes. Such was the reality for Margaret de Holland, who in 1305 and 1307 made petitions in Parliament regarding a range of disputes over her deceased husband John's accumulated debts as collector of a series of royal taxes in Lincolnshire under Edward I.[18]

That women felt a sense of ownership of the idea of their own fiscal responsibilities is strongly suggested by a petition to the king and Council in Parliament in *c.* 1321, in which Agnes la Clerke of Ogbourne complained of the theft of five quarters of wheat which she had been taking from Marlborough to Salisbury to sell; her assailants had beaten and wounded her and broken her arm. La Clerke specified that the planned sale of goods had been occasioned by her need for money to pay the tax of a fifteenth (probably the parliamentary grant of 1316) and other unspecified contributions to the king. Agnes la Clerke's legal advisers were obviously highly adept: by demonstrating her commitment to the public obligation of taxation, she might be able to catch the ears of the triers of petitions. The response suggests that this was indeed so. It was judged that, if the trespasses were as bad as the petition alleged, then Agnes should be allowed a special commission of oyer and terminer to investigate the whole matter.[19]

The same sense of confidence in the face of officialdom is evident in some of the petitions that women submitted in Parliament requesting recovery of debts owed to them by the Crown.[20] Denise Lymbrennere of London complained in 1322 that she was still owed for lime provided towards the decoration of Westminster Palace for Edward II's coronation back in 1308.[21] About the same, time, Alice, the widow of Robert le Taillour, tailor to Edward I, complained that she was still owed money on unsettled bills with king's Wardrobe stretching back to the 1290s.[22] Similarly, early in Edward III's reign, Alice Sperwe, evidently a brewer in Southwark, complained that she had been unable to recover a debt of over £12 for ale supplied to Edward III's household when he was earl of Chester. Alice's petition added a fairly conventional plea: the king should remedy this wrong for God, and for his father's soul, lest Alice herself be 'destroyed and impoverished' (*anencie et enpoverie*).[23]

Sometimes in such cases, however, women could be quite outspoken. Emmotte, the widow of John Esmond, a London goldsmith, petitioned in the Leicester Parliament of 1426 concerning debts owed to her by the Crown for new and reworked seals provided by her late husband to Henry IV on the occasion of the latter's change to the royal arms in 1406.[24] Emmotte claimed that the former king had expressly ordered the seals from John by word of mouth at a meeting in the royal chamber, with the result there was no documentation of the transaction and that the Exchequer would therefore now give no credence to her claim. What is particularly remarkable about Emmotte's petition is the way in which she was able to reference authorities in defence of her case. She claimed that the bishop of Durham (Thomas Langley), Sir John Pelham and other knights of the chamber to Henry IV knew the circumstances well. Both Langley and Pelham were executors of Henry IV's will. It may have been as a result of consultation with them, or with some other courtier or royal official, that Emmotte was also able to state authoritatively, 'as by the parliament rolls of the said Parliament [of 1422] plainly appears' (*sicome par les rolles du dit parlement pleinement appiert*), that she ought already to have been reimbursed under the arrangements made at the beginning of Henry VI's reign for the settlement of the personal estates of Henry IV and Henry V.[25] Now, in 1426, having failed to get satisfaction from Henry IV's executors, Emmotte put herself upon the good services of the Lords in the hope that her case could be addressed in Parliament and proper payment authorised.

The ways in which Emmotte Esmond aimed to work the system of petitioning in Parliament may not have been wholly successful—there is no recorded action upon her petition of 1426—but they demonstrate that women of her status were far from intimidated by the political and legal institutions based at Westminster and could navigate a course perfectly well around those influential courtiers and Lords who might speak in their support. Her case, and others described in this and previous chapters, provides strong support to the need, indentified by Tanner, Gathagan and

Huneycutt, for a new conceptual model of women's place in the structures and discourses of power during the Middle Ages. No longer is it adequate to treat cases like that of Emmotte Esmond as entertaining sidelights interesting only for their exceptionality and accompanying oddity. Rather, we need to speak truth to cases such as these and assert that the female lobbyist could indeed be a political reality in fifteenth-century England.

Notes

1. Scott, 'Gender' (quote at 1073).
2. Tanner, Gathagan and Huneycutt, 'Introduction' (quote at 6).
3. SC 8/24/1165, printed from the original in *RP*, IV, 158. The summary in *PROME*, IX, 310 is misleading on women.
4. For women physicians, see Talbot and Hammond, *Medical Practitioners*, 10, 28, 100, 200, 209, 211; and Green, 'Women's Medical Practice', 440.
5. C 65/82, m. 15, printed in *RP*, IV, 130, and in *PROME*, IX, 267–8.
6. Putnam, *Enforcement of the Statute of Labourers*, Appendix, 8–12; C 65/15, m. 1, printed in *RP*, II, 233–4, and in *PROME*, V, 28; *SR*, I, 311.
7. C 65/21, m. 3, printed in *RP*, II, 277–8, and in *PROME*, V, 164–5; *SR*, I, 379–80; Gastle, '"As if she were single"'.
8. Hector and Harvey, eds, *Westminster Chronicle*, 356–68, reproduced in *PROME*, VII, 124–5; *SR*, II, 57.
9. C 65/97, m. 4, printed in *RP*, V, 112–13, and in *PROME*, XI, 492–4; *SR*, II, 338.
10. Graham, '"A woman's work ..."'; Bardsley, 'Women's Work Reconsidered'; Bennett, *History Matters*, 82–107; Humphries and Weisdorf, 'Wages of Women'.
11. Harriss, *King, Parliament and Public Finance.*
12. Willard, *Parliamentary Taxes.*
13. Dyer, 'Taxation and Communities'.
14. For the clauses in the tax grants of 1377, 1379 and 1380 specifying the inclusion of women, see C 65/31, m. 8, printed in *RP*, II, 364, and in *PROME*, V, 400; C 65/34, mm. 7-6, printed in *RP*, III, 58–9, and in *PROME*, VI, 114–16; C 65/36, m. 5, printed in *RP*, III, 89–90, and in *PROME*, VI, 190–2. For the importance of the poll taxes as a source for the history of *femmes soles*, see Goldberg, 'Urban Identity', 194–216; and Beattie, *Medieval Single Women*, 62–95.
15. Ormrod, 'Poverty and Privilege'. Archer, '"How ladies ... who live on their manors ought to manage their households and estates"', 162–4, calculates that a third of landed wealth liable to the income tax of 1436 was

held by women. For women recorded in the alien subsidy returns, see Ruddick, 'Immigrants and Intermarriage'.

16. For women's participation in the Peasants' Revolt, see Federico, 'The Imaginary Society', esp. 165–9.
17. Ormrod, *Political Life*, 42, 90–2.
18. 1305: SC 8/266/13272, printed in Maitland, ed., *Memoranda de Parliamento*, 71, and (with supporting contextual material) in *PROME*, II, 218–19. 1307: SC 8/2/55, printed in *RP*, I, 205–6, and dated in *PROME*, II, 564–5.
19. SC 8/39/1942.
20. For the frequency of such petitions by men, as well as by women, see Brand, 'Understanding Early Petitions', 109–10.
21. SC 8/6/287, printed in *RP*, I, 406.
22. SC 8/144/7198.
23. SC 8/72/3562. For an earlier petition from Margery de Jernemuth submitted in the later years of Edward II and referencing debts owed to her for provisions supplied to the king's household stretching back as far as Edward I's visit to Ghent in 1297, see SC 8/118/5873. This was sent directly before the king (*Coram domino regis*), but the outcome is unknown.
24. SC 8/25/1210, printed in *RP*, IV, 312. For Esmond's responsibility for the new great seal of 1406, see Cherry, 'Some Lancastrian Seals', 20–2.
25. For the relevant entry on the parliament roll of November 1422, see C 65/84, mm. 12–11, printed in *RP*, IV, 172–3, and in *PROME*, X, 19–21; Strong and Strong, 'Last Will and Codicils of Henry V', 86–7. For Pelham's career, see Lock, 'Pelham, Sir John'.

References

Unpublished Primary Sources

Kew, The National Archives of the United Kingdom

C 65 Chancery: Parliament Rolls.

SC 8 Special Collections: Ancient Petitions.

Published Primary Sources

Brand, Paul, Seymour Phillips, W. Mark Ormrod, Geoffrey Martin, Chris Given Wilson, Anne Curry and Rosemary Horrox, eds, *The Parliament Rolls of Medieval England*, 16 vols (Woodbridge: Boydell, 2005).

Maitland, Frederic W., ed., *Memoranda de Parliamento, 1305*, Rolls Series 98 (London, 1893).

Raithby, John, ed., *The Statutes of the Realm*, 11 vols (London: Record Commission, 1810–1828).

Strachey, J., ed., *Rotuli Parliamentorum*, 6 vols (London: Record Commission, 1767–1777).

Published Secondary Sources

Archer, Rowena E., '"How ladies … who live on their manors ought to manage their households and estates": Women as Landholders and Administrators in the Later Middle Ages', in *Women in Medieval English Society, c. 1200–c. 1500*, ed. P. J. P. Goldberg (Stroud: Sutton, 1997), 149–81.

Bardsley, Sandy, 'Women's Work Reconsidered: Gender and Wage Differentiation in Late Medieval England', *Past & Present* 165 (1999): 3–29.

Beattie, Cordelia, *Medieval Single Women: The Politics of Social Classification in Late Medieval England* (Oxford: Oxford University Press, 2007).

Cherry, John, 'Some Lancastrian Seals', in *The Lancastrian Court*, ed. Jenny Stratford (Donington: Shaun Tyas, 2003), 19–28.

Dyer, Christopher, 'Taxation and Communities in Late Medieval England', in *Progress and Problems in Medieval England: Essays in Honour of Edward Miller*, ed. Richard H. Britnell and John Hatcher (Cambridge: Cambridge University Press, 1996), 168–90.

Federico, Sylvia, 'The Imaginary Society: Women in 1381', *Journal of British Studies* 40 (2001): 159–83.

Gastle, Brian W., '"As if she were single": Working Wives and the Late Medieval *Femme Sole*', in *The Middle Ages at Work: Practicing Labour in Late Medieval England*, ed. Kellie Robertson and Michael Uebel (Basingstoke: Palgrave Macmillan, 2004), 41–64.

Goldberg, P. J. P., 'Urban Identity and the Poll Taxes of 1377, 1379 and 1381', *Economic History Review* 2nd ser. 43 (1990): 194–216.

Graham, Helena, '"A woman's work …": Labour and Gender in the Late Medieval Countryside', in *Women in Medieval English Society, c. 1200–c. 1500*, ed. P. J. P. Goldberg (Stroud: Sutton, 1997), 126–48.

Green, Monica H., 'Women's Medical Practice and Health Care in Medieval Europe', *Signs* 14 (1988–1989): 434–73.

Harriss, G. L., *King, Parliament and Public Finance in Medieval England to 1369* (Oxford: Oxford University Press, 1975).

Humphries, Jane and Jacob Weisdorf, 'The Wages of Women in England, 1260–1850', *Journal of Economic History* 75 (2015): 405–47.

Lock, Julian, 'Pelham, Sir John', in *The Oxford Dictionary of National Biography*, ed. H. C. G. Matthew and Brian H. Harrison (Oxford: Oxford University Press, 2004), XLIII, 470.

Ormrod, W. Mark, *Political Life in England, 1300–1450* (Basingstoke: Macmillan, 1995).

Ormrod, W. Mark, 'Poverty and Privilege: The Fiscal Burden in England (XIIIth–XVth Centuries)', in *Fiscal Systems in the European Economy from the 13th to the 18th Centuries*, ed. Simonetta Cavaciocchi (Florence: University of Florence Press, 2008), 637–56.

Putnam, Bertha H., *The Enforcement of the Statute of Labourers during the First Decade after the Black Death, 1349–1359* (New York: Columbia University Press, 1908).

Ruddick, Andrea, 'Immigrants and Intermarriage in Late Medieval England', in *Resident Aliens in Later Medieval England*, ed. W. Mark Ormrod, Nicola McDonald and Craig Taylor (Turnhout: Brepols, 2017), 181–200.

Scott, Joan, 'Gender: A Useful Category of Historical Analysis', *American Historical Review* 91 (1986): 1053–75.

Strong, Patrick, and Felicity Strong, 'The Last Will and Codicils of Henry V', *English Historical Review* 96 (1981): 79–102.

Talbot, C. H. and E. A. Hammond, *The Medical Practitioners of Medieval England: A Biographical Register* (London: Wellcome Historical Medical Library, 1965).

Tanner, Heather J., Laura L. Gathagan and Lois L. Huneycutt, 'Introduction', in *Medieval Elite Women and the Exercise of Power, 1100–1400: Moving Beyond the Exceptionalist Debate*, ed. Heather J. Tanner (Basingstoke: Palgrave Macmillan, 2019), 1–18.

CHAPTER 9

Conclusion: Women Speaking Out in the Medieval Parliament

Abstract The concluding chapter analyses an unusual case from the Parliament of 1427–1428 in which a group of London women were said to have entered the meeting-place of Parliament at Westminster Palace and protested (in written form) against the actions of the Duke of Gloucester in divorcing his wife and taking his mistress as his bride. The case is suggestive of women, in various groupings and collectives, campaigning on certain moral issues during the later Middle Ages. The chapter then moves back to the question of agency, raised in the Introduction, and considers a small number of cases from the time of Edward I in which female petitioners deployed letter-writing forms in addressing the king directly and expressing their grievances in the first-person singular. (Petitions, by contrast, were normally written in the third person.) This evidence suggests, again, that women played an active part in raising moral issues within the predominantly male forum of Parliament.

Keywords Agency • Emotion • Gender • Life-writing • Parliament

W. M. Ormrod, *Women and Parliament in Later Medieval England*, The New Middle Ages,
https://doi.org/10.1007/978-3-030-45220-9_9

The Women of London

In his account of the 1427–1428 Parliament at Westminster, the St Albans monk, John of Amundesham, provided the story of an unusual incident otherwise unreferenced either in the official records of Parliament or in other chronicles:

> In this Parliament, a certain woman of the Stocks Market came openly into Parliament with certain other women of London, respectfully attired, bearing letters to the duke of Gloucester, the archbishops and the other Lords there present. The tenor of these letters was to reproach the duke of Gloucester on account of his refusal to rescue his wife from her effective imprisonment by the duke of Burgundy. Rather, as his love for her had grown cold, he was inclined to leave her in captivity, and he was holding himself for another in adultery and quite publicly so, to the ruin of himself, of the realm and of the strength of the institution of marriage.[1]

This episode derives some credibility from the fact that the mayor, aldermen and commonalty of the city of London are known to have sent their own representation to Parliament, protesting at the treatment of the duke of Gloucester's wife, Jacqueline of Hainault.[2] Duke Humphrey had married Jacqueline in 1423 after she had sought refuge in England from her husband, John IV, duke of Brabant. For some while, and with the support of the English Crown, Gloucester had pursued Jacqueline's rights as heiress to Hainault, Holland and Zeeland, but had already lost interest in the benefits of the marriage before January 1428 when the pope (in spite of John of Brabant's death) finally confirmed that Humphrey's marriage with Jacqueline was invalid.[3] The protest of the London women is therefore likely to have been in concert with that of the city authorities, in the wake of the news of the effective annulment of Gloucester's marriage at the end of the second session of the Parliament in March 1428.[4]

Reading the above passage from Amundesham in the light of the foregoing discussion of the role of women in the later medieval English Parliament provides the opportunity both for a new evaluation of this alleged episode and for some wider concluding generalisations about women's place in Parliament. Earlier, in Chap. 5, we had occasion to doubt the agency of women in a series of fourteenth-century petitions expressed in the name of the 'women of London' or 'widows of London'. In some of these instances at least, the petitions can be seen as crafted by men in order to drive home the relevance of the given issue to female, as well as male, inhabitants of the city and thus, in a sense, to cover all bases. However, we have also seen that individual women could push at the boundaries of the law and stretch parliamentary process in order to raise more general points of concern shared with men, such as dower, rape and the Crown's debts. Gloucester's betrayal of his marriage vows to Jacqueline of Hainault involved not one offence against womankind but three: leaving his wife stranded on the continent, under duress from the duke of Burgundy; not responding to the papal annulment by seeking to honour Jacqueline's virtue and going through a second, valid, marriage ceremony with her; and humiliating her by choosing immediately to take as his new bride his mistress, Eleanor Cobham.[5] In the face of this triple scandal, it is perhaps reasonable to suggest that the authorities in the city of London felt it entirely appropriate that their remonstration, which could be construed as primarily concerned with the risks posed to English foreign policy, might be matched by a protest from womenfolk invested in the social conventions of marriage.

Accessing Royal Grace

The London women's protest of 1428 was clearly an exceptional event prompted by an unusual set of circumstances. It is a reflection of the sensitivities around the fate of Jacqueline of Hainault that the authorities of London chose not to submit a petition to the Commons and Lords of Parliament, as would have been conventional at this time, but instead sent the recorder of the city to address the Lords and Commons *viva voce*. Amundesham has the women of London also appear before Parliament, but claims that they made their remonstrance in the form of written letters (*litterae*). We should not over-interpret the chronicler's choice of words, but these letters were arguably different both in form and in content from the ordinary type of petition (*petitio* or *billa* in Latin; *petition* or *bille* in Anglo-Norman French) with which this study has been mainly concerned.[6] The letter form, we may suggest, was chosen consciously in order to differentiate this matter from the normal, public business of Parliament, and to give a particular effect—of authenticity and authority, of agency and urgency—to the complaint. The incident of 1428 therefore serves to foreground two major issues in women's relationship with the later medieval English Parliament: the difficulty of gaining personal access to the chambers in which the work of Parliament was undertaken; and the problem of ensuring that grievances communicated in writing were attended to and acted upon efficiently and effectively.

In what has gone before, we have noted just five cases in which women (other than queens) seem to have appeared in person in Parliament: Alice Perrers' trial of 1377; the process upon Alice de Neville's petition on behalf of her granddaughter in 1378; the audience of Margaret Basset's petition against Richard Stanhope in 1414; the upbraiding of the duke of Gloucester by a group of London women in 1428; and (possibly) the duchess of York's dramatic supplication for her husband in 1459.[7] If the clerks of Parliament and the chroniclers had been less laconic in their official and unofficial accounts of more of the sessions that sat from the later thirteenth to the later fifteenth century, we would no doubt have more instances and a surer basis on which to list women's personal appearances in Parliament. Even so, it remains an undoubted reality that the vast majority of women who had business in Parliament did so at several removes.

There was nothing especially gendered about this position, of course: most of the thousands of petitions submitted by men, and male collectives, in Parliament were also submitted by legal agents, and sometimes by MPs themselves.[8] Nor does the preceding analysis throw up any particular suggestion that women were systemically disadvantaged by the ways in which their (male) legal advisers and the (male) committees of triers in Parliament communicated and judged their cases. As Jeremy Goldberg has found for the church courts, so also apparently in Parliament: there was no observable difference between the treatment of women's and men's cases, and no sense in which women's evidence was treated as inferior to men's.[9] Thus when Joan Ippegrave was rebuffed in Parliament in 1290 for her failure to specify whether her petition had referred to her claimed rights in Old or New Winchelsea, the Crown was simply upholding a level of precision that it would also have applied to men.[10] Similarly, the carefully argued case of Joan, widow of Ralph Basset of Drayton, in 1346, that a special commission of oyer and terminer issued against her should be withdrawn as being incompatible with statute law, was dismissed with the same reasoning that would have been applied to a male supplicant: such commissions, once issued, could not be repealed in this manner.[11]

That women were generally deprived of the opportunity to appear in person in Parliament does, however, raise particular questions about the triangular relationship between the female supplicant, her scrivener and/or attorney, and those who judged her case in Parliament (the committees of triers or the king and Council).[12] To have a petition accepted also required the intervention of the clerks of Parliament (drawn from the royal Chancery), who sorted petitions at the point of submission and seem to have been responsible for reading them aloud before the triers or the Council and making the endorsements that recorded the judgment on the case.[13] The oral/aural nature of the process is one important reason why women's petitions, like men's, used rhetorical devices to attract attention to their causes and secure favourable responses.[14] We have already pointed to the tropes of poverty and defencelessness as ones that petitions from women were especially inclined to adopt as a means of attracting sympathy. One further, exceptional, strategy forms a fitting coda to the current study: the use of the first person in appeals intended directly for the king's ears.

First-Person Narratives

It was an important element of the conventions of medieval letter-writing that the use of the first person for the addresser and the second person for the addressee (either singular or plural, depending on whether they were equals or superiors) created a sense of immediacy, intimacy and trust.[15] We have already noted the use of the first-person form in the final section of the 1355 petition of Blanche, Lady Wake.[16] Two other examples, both dating from the late thirteenth century, make more general use of this technique. The first of these, which has about half of the original document torn away and is only impressionistically datable to the reign of Edward I, is from Sybil de la Mare.[17] Sybil had a grievance against the family of one Philip Marmyun, who had launched a claim to land that Sybil regarded as part of the inheritance of her son (unnamed in the surviving portions of the document): '***I*** have a son who is the right heir … And that ***you*** do not suffer ***my*** son to be disinherited … (*ieo* ***ay*** *un fiz ke est drayt heyre … Et ke* ***ws*** [i.e. "vous"] *ne soffrez ke* ***mun*** *fiz ne seyt deserite …*)' (emphases added). The surviving fragment has no endorsement and we have no known provenance for the document, although it sits within the section of the Ancient Petitions that follows on immediately from the 'Parliamentary Petitions' and which, in Dodd's view, represents a continuous run of documents likely to have been submitted in Parliament.[18] The use of the first and second persons might suggest a scribe who did not know all the conventions of petitioning, such as they had developed at this stage. The characteristic opening of the petition, 'Sybil de la Mare shows

you that …' (*Ceo* ***ws*** *moustre Sibile de la Mare ke* …) (emphasis added) is certainly found in other petitions of the reign of Edward I, and specifically from the Parliament of 1290; it may be that the use of the second person in the address clause encouraged the scribe to fall into the first person for the description of Sybil's grievance. Other petitions using this opening form, did not, however, divert from the strict use of the third person in relation to the petitioner.[19] Sybil's desire, or her clerk's decision, to express her petition in the first-person singular may therefore reflect the particular anxiety that the petitioner felt around the case and an understanding that this unusual form might itself attract attention to her plaint.

It is our final example of a petition deploying the first and second person forms that may bring us closest to the actual words spoken by the original petitioner.[20] In 1290, the king and Council in Parliament received and processed a petition that begins as follows:

> To our lord the king, Contessa, late the wife of Roger de Clifford, prays … that because she has been grievously distrained by his sheriffs for various debts of her husband Roger de Clifford …[21]

So far, so normal: by 1290 'to our lord the king' (along with 'to our lord the king and his Council') had become the default form of opening for a petition, and Contessa's scribe faithfully followed the convention, in the opening section, of referring to both the petitioner and the king in the third person.[22] However, the voice then immediately shifts into the first-person singular, with the addressee, the king, taking the (plural and formal) second person or (singular and intimate) third person according to context:

> … and ***I*** [am] not … [her deceased husband, Roger's] heir nor [do I] have anything except through our lord the king, and this at the term of ***my*** life; and [I] pray the king's grace, since it is through ***him*** that ***I*** have [what I have], for ***I*** do not have … the lands to hold to render his debt. So ***I*** pray ***you***, dear lord, … grace.[23]

Contessa Clifford was the second wife of Sir Roger Clifford (d. before 1286), whose son by his first wife, also named Roger (d. 1314), was the first member of the family to be raised to the parliamentary peerage. The elder and younger Rogers were both close associates of Edward I; Roger the elder had served with the king while he was prince and had accompanied him on crusade in 1270–1272. The marriage to Contessa is said to have taken place while Roger was returning home from crusade through France. Both contemporary and later sources assume from various garbled versions of her name that she was the 'countess of Lerett', or 'Lauretania'.[24] Although this title remains, in Kathryn Faulkner's words, 'obstinately impenetrable', it is clear that Contessa was of foreign extraction, since her possessions were subjected to the confiscation of aliens' property on the outbreak of war with France in 1294, and were subsequently restored to her on the order of the king.[25] Whatever her precise origins, it is clear that Contessa felt that her station in life, her late husband's proximity to the king, and her own record as a beneficiary of gifts from the Crown, allowed her to address Edward I both with intimacy and with forthrightness.[26] It is not just the use of the personal forms that marks her 1290 petition out as rather unusual. The references to her total dependence on the gift or grace of the king (twice) and the unusual mention of her old age and impending mortality also have the effect of lifting the rhetoric well above the more general pleas of poverty and helplessness that we have seen on the part of other women supplicants. Taken together, these features of Contessa's petition render the text, like the last part of Blanche Wake's petition of 1355, much more like a private letter (and a piece of life-writing) than a petition lodged in Parliament.

Contessa got her way. The endorsement to her petition, and the note of the decision made on the parliament roll for 1290, indicate the firm intention of the king and Council that she was not to be distrained for the debts of her husband, unless she happened to be his executrix and therefore responsible for his liabilities.[27] The rhetorical strategy had paid off, and the attention of the Crown had been won. We could build a whole micro-history around this incident in the life of Contessa de Clifford, in which the self-conscious confidence of a lady asserting her own status in the imagined presence of the king creates a telling tale of female agency in the patriarchal world of parliamentary politics. The cases in which women used the first-person form of address in parliamentary petitions may be highly exceptional, but they are all the more remarkable given that men did not resort to such strategies. The only petition addressed by men where I have been able to locate a shift from the third person to the first and second persons is one of *c.* 1308, addressed by the king's bailiffs of the town of Ipswich (who therefore used the first-person plural).[28] Like those of Sybil de la Mare and Contessa Clifford, it belongs to an early period in the development of petitionary form: in this sense, all three such examples indicate a certain latitude that no longer existed, either for men or for women, once the full conventions around the writing of petitions developed over the first quarter of the fourteenth century. If that point is correct, however, then it also throws into sharper relief the confident temerity with which Blanche Wake made her own personal appeal to Edward III in 1355.

For every Lady Clifford and Lady Wake, of course, there were hundreds of women of middling and lower status in each generation who could not assert a special relationship with the king, and who had to depend not on unusual discursive strategies but on the force and worth of their own cases to work within the system and achieve a hearing in Parliament. The particular interest that attaches to the cases of Sybil de la Mare, Contessa Clifford and Blanche Wake, however, relates to the issue raised in Chap. 1 about women's agency. Investigation of the ways in which the wayward narratives of women's quarrels were manipulated by those with legal knowhow into conventional forms that fitted the requirements of the courts has led to an understanding that the resulting written evidence is, to an extent, a fiction, and that we cannot appreciate the truth of a given case unless we find ways in which to identify the authentic voice of the female supplicant. We have seen some kind of truth emerging from the documentation in a number of ways: when women directed their petitions to the Commons so as to open up a wider debate on the topic and have it adopted as one of the common petitions; in cases where a woman's accusations take on an unusual specificity and/or cross-refer to other evidence, including the parliament rolls; and in those instances where women self-consciously went beyond the bounds of the law to argue for a form of natural justice obtainable only through the dispensation of royal grace. The use of the first person in petitions to the Crown in Parliament allows us to imagine the authentic female voice 'ventriloquised' (to use Jeremy Goldberg's term) by the Chancery clerks who read petitions aloud to the committees of triers, to the Commons or Lords, and to the king and Council.[29] The collective effect of such hearings allowed women's causes to be taken up and prosecuted actively by men in Parliament, whether in the sponsoring of a private petition through the Commons or even, in some cases, through successful requests for legislation upon test cases, designed for the general good.

Conclusion

This study has shown that quite significant numbers of women, of varied social ranks, used the parliamentary process of private petitioning throughout the later Middle Ages as a means of highlighting their individual grievances and, in the process, asserting their collective rights. If Parliament was not an institution that allowed women's direct presence in the Commons or the Lords, it was still a venue in which women could get their voices heard and sometimes, at least, have their concerns answered. We have seen that women could freely petition in Parliament under the conventions that allowed independent females (*femmes soles*) to undertake their own representation in legal cases. But we have also seen that, because Parliament operated outside the restrictions of the common law, married women could also, under some circumstances, lay forth their grievances there. Reflecting on the restricted opportunities that women had to operate as lay collectives, we have nonetheless seen that the idea and/or the reality of what might almost be called 'women's movements' existed in some of the supplicatory representations of the women of London. In spite of laws which claimed that noblewomen who rebelled against the Crown should be tried there, Parliament did not generally undertake public trials of women, but instead used the emerging process of attainder to pass acts against male and female members of the aristocracy alike; only in the very unusual case of Alice Perrers was a woman actually brought into Parliament and put to trial for high crimes against the Crown. In relation to the politics of dower, we have seen that women's petitions constructed novel and persistent (if ultimately unsuccessful) arguments about the non-liability of wives to the punishments meted out against those men who rebelled against the Crown. And in connection with the other major 'women's issue' raised here, rape, it has been argued that petitions submitted by women in Parliament helped to reinforce the abhorrence that was articulated by men in the common petitions and anti-rape legislation, and thus gave the public debates on rape a moral, rather than merely a material, dimension. These cases, and others, have also served to question more broadly the idea that the law of coverture and patriarchal social conventions prevented women—even, sometimes, married women—from having their say, and getting their way, in the masculine world of later medieval parliamentary politics.

Notes

1. Amundesham, *Annales*, I, 20, translated in *PROME*, X, 365: 'In hoc quoque parliamento, quaedam mulierum de Stokkes venit palam in parliamento, cum quibusdam aliis foeminis Londoniarum, reverenter ornatis, porrigens litteras duci Gloverniae, archiepiscopis, caeterisque dominis ibidem existentibus; et tenor litterarum erat increpatorius penes ducem Gloverniae, nolentam suam uxorem ab eflictione cercali ducens Borgundiae eripere, sed, amore refrigerato, sic in servitute permanere sinere; et quod aliam, adulteram, publice secum tenuerit, suae personae, regni ruinae, et sponsalis ordinis efficaciae.'
2. Amundesham, *Annales*, I, 18; Sharpe, ed., *Calendar of Letter Books*, XI (Letter Book K), 68; Myers, 'Parliamentary Petitions', 386; and summary of the foregoing sources in *PROME*, X, 367.
3. Harriss, 'Humphrey, Duke of Gloucester', 788–9.
4. See the discussion in *PROME*, X, 321.
5. Harriss, 'Eleanor (née Eleanor Cobham), Duchess of Gloucester'. For Eleanor's subsequent trial for sorcery, see above, 58–59.
6. For the forms of letters and petitions, see above, 37n41.
7. See above, 28–29, 46–48, 54–57, 101, 126–127.
8. Maddicott, 'Parliament and the Constituencies'.
9. Goldberg, 'Gender and Matrimonial Litigation'.
10. SC 8/266/13269, transcribed and translated in *PROME*, I, 376, 422.
11. SC 8/32/1551. The relevant commission is *CPR, 1345–8*, 183.
12. For the range of paralegal services available to women (and men) preparing suits at law, see Ramsay, 'Retained Legal Counsel'; Ramsay, 'Scriveners and Notaries'; Musson, *Medieval Law in Context*, 36–83; Bevan, 'Clerks and Scriveners'. For evidence of the writing of petitions by professionals, see Dodd, *Justice and Grace*, 302–14; Killick, 'Treason, Felony and Lollardy'.
13. For the influence of Chancery clerks over the business of Parliament, see Pollard, 'Clerical Organisation of Parliament'; Pollard, 'Receivers of Petitions and Clerks of Parliament'; Pollard, 'Clerk of the Crown'; Cuttino, 'King's Clerks', 404–6; Bradford and McHardy, eds, *Proctors for Parliament*, II, xxii–xxviii.
14. For further discussion, see Ormrod, 'Murmur, Clamour and Noise'.
15. For the self-conscious use of the first-person singular, see Glenda McLeod, '"Wholly guilty, wholly innocent"', 65–6.
16. See above, 32–33.
17. SC 8/200/9952. The recoverable text reads as follows: 'Ceo ws moustre Sibile de la Mare ke Filipp' Marmyun … vindrint les filles le auant dite Philipp' e lur baruns … Philipp' vint le Chetur nostre seignur le Rey de Wiltesyr' … lies e lur baruns. E dite ke Philipp' tinte un verge de … est

prise[?] ke rien ne tinte de Ray en chef. Parunt leo ws pri … de cel tere si come ieo ay un fiz ke est drayt heyre … suyr. E ke ws ne doffrez ke mun fiz ne seyt deserite ….' I am grateful to Shelagh Sneddon for assistance with this transcription.

18. See above, 8.
19. SC 8/50/2474, printed in *PROME*, I, 354; SC 8/120/5971, printed in *PROME*, I, 362; SC 8/308/15381, printed in *PROME*, I, 374. These three instances are noted by Brand, 'Petitions and Parliament', 25. See also SC 8/1/5 and an alternative version at SC 8/219/10915, both printed in *PROME*, I, 363. The form had apparently disappeared by 1305: Brand, 'Petitions and Parliament', 26.
20. For what follows, see SC 8/219/10916. I rely partly on the edition and translation in *PROME*, I, 370, 416, but have amended the translation in light of close reading. The question of recovering the authentic voice from legal and paralegal sources has provoked lively debate, and the development of some sophisticated methodologies, especially with regard to the work of the church courts. See, within a much larger bibliography: Goldberg, 'Fiction in the Archives'; Hanawalt, *'Of Good and Ill Repute'*, 124–41; Musson, 'Crossing Boundaries'; McSheffrey, 'Detective Fiction in the Archives'; Goldberg, 'Echoes, Whispers, Ventriloquisms'; Kane, 'Women, Memory and Agency', 43–62.
21. 'A noster seyngnur le ray prie Cuntasse ke fu la femme Roger de Clifford … kar ele est destreynd par ces vicuntes grevosement pur deverce dettes sun seyngur Roger de Clifford ….'
22. For address clauses in 1290, see Brand, 'Petitions in Parliament', 25–6.
23. '… e jeo ne … sun eir new reyn ne ay fur ke par noster seyngnur le ray e ceo a terme de ma vie; e prie la grace le ray sicum ceo est par li co ke jeo naveray …ener les teres a tenir a render sa dette. Dunt jeo ws prie, cher seygnur, … grace.' Emphases added in translation.
24. Cokayne, *Complete Peerage*, III, 290; Kathryn 'Clifford, Sir Roger de'.
25. Faulkner, 'Clifford, Sir Roger de', 110; *CCR, 1288–96*, 234. Contessa had been out of the country at the time of the initial seizure in 1294 and remained abroad for most of the 1290s: *CPR, 1292–1301*, 140, 381; *CCR, 1296–1302*, 342. For the background to the seizure of aliens' property, see Lambert and Ormrod, 'A Matter of Trust', 212–15.
26. For Edward I's gifts to Contessa of wood from the king's forests in 1278–1279, see *CCR, 1272–9*, 450, 518.
27. C 65/2, m. 3d, printed in *RP*, I, 53, and in *PROME*, I, 313; SC 8/219/10916, printed in *PROME*, I, 370 and translated in *PROME*, I, 416.
28. SC 8/49/2414, calendared in Joseph Bain, ed., *Calendar of Documents*, 47. SC 8/66/3260G contains a first-person address, but is a memoran-

dum subordinate to a petition, rather than a petition itself: see Ormrod, 'Memory, Genealogy and Nationality', 88.

29. Goldberg, 'Echoes, Whispers, Ventriloquisms', 31.

References

Unpublished Primary Sources

Kew, The National Archives of the United Kingdom

C 65 Chancery: Parliament Rolls.

SC 8 Special Collections: Ancient Petitions.

Published Primary Sources

Amundesham, John, *Annales Monasterii S. Albani (A.D. 1421–1440)*, ed. Henry T. Riley, 2 vols, Rolls Series 28[5] (London, 1870–1871).

Bain, Joseph, ed., *Calendar of Documents Relating to Scotland, III: 1307–1357* (Edinburgh: Her Majesty's General Register House, 1888).

Bradford, Phil, and Alison K. McHardy, eds, *Proctors for Parliament: Clergy, Community and Politics, c. 1248–1539*, 2 vols, Canterbury and York Society 107–8 (Woodbridge, 2017–2018).

Brand, Paul, Seymour Phillips, W. Mark Ormrod, Geoffrey Martin, Chris Given Wilson, Anne Curry and Rosemary Horrox, eds, *The Parliament Rolls of Medieval England*, 16 vols (Woodbridge: Boydell, 2005).

Calendar of the Close Rolls Preserved in the Public Record Office, Henry III-Henry VII, 61 vols (London: Her/His Majesty's Stationery Office, 1892–1963).

Calendar of the Patent Rolls Preserved in the Public Record Office, Henry III–Henry VII, 54 vols (London: Her/His Majesty's Stationery Office, 1891–1916).

Sharpe, Reginald R., ed., *Calendar of the Letter Books of the City of London*, 12 vols (London: Her/His Majesty's Stationery Office, 1899–1912).

Strachey, J., ed., *Rotuli Parliamentorum*, 6 vols (London: Record Commission, 1767–1777).

Published Secondary Sources

Brand, Paul, 'Petitions and Parliament in the Reign of Edward I', *Parliamentary History* 23 (2004): 14–38.

Cuttino, G. P., 'King's Clerks and the Community of the Realm', *Speculum* 29 (1954): 395–409.

Dodd, Gwilym, *Justice and Grace: Private Petitioning and the English Parliament in the Late Middle Ages* (Oxford: Oxford University Press, 2007).

Faulkner, Kathryn, 'Clifford, Sir Roger de', in *Oxford Dictionary of National Biography*, ed. H. C. G. Matthew and Brian H. Harrison, 60 vols (Oxford: Oxford University Press, 2004), XII, 109–10.

Goldberg, P. J. P., 'Echoes, Whispers, Ventriloquisms: On Recovering Women's Voices from the Court of York in the Later Middle Ages', in *Women, Agency and the Law, 1300–1700*, ed. Bronach Kane and Fiona Williamson, The Body, Gender and Culture 15 (London: Taylor & Francis, 2013), 31–41.

Goldberg, P. J. P., 'Fiction in the Archives: The York Cause Papers as a Source for Later Medieval Social History', *Continuity and Change* 12 (1997): 425–45.

Goldberg, P. J. P., 'Gender and Matrimonial Litigation in the Church Courts in the Later Middle Ages: The Evidence of the Court of York', *Gender and History* 19 (2007): 43–59.

Hanawalt, Barbara A., *'Of Good and Ill Repute': Gender and Social Control in Medieval England* (Oxford: Oxford University Press, 1998).

Harriss, G. L., 'Eleanor (née Eleanor Cobham), Duchess of Gloucester', in *The Oxford Dictionary of National Biography*, ed. H. C. G. Matthew and Brian H. Harrison, 60 vols (Oxford: Oxford University Press, 2004a), XVIII, 27–8.

Harriss, G. L., 'Humphrey, Duke of Gloucester', in *The Oxford Dictionary of National Biography*, ed. H. C. G. Matthew, H. C. G. and Brian H. Harrison (Oxford: Oxford University Press, 2004b), XXVIII, 787–93.

Kane, Bronach, 'Women, Memory and Agency in the Medieval English Church Courts', in Bronach Kane and Fiona Williamson, eds, *Women, Agency and the Law, 1300–1700*, The Body, Gender and Culture 15 (London: Taylor & Francis, 2013), 43–62.

Killick, Helen, 'Treason, Felony and Lollardy: A Common Petition in the Hand of Richard Osbarn, Clerk of the Chamber of the Guildhall, 1400–*c.* 1437', *Historical Research* 89 (2016): 227–45.

Lambert, Bart and W. Mark Ormrod, 'A Matter of Trust: The Royal Regulation of England's French Residents during Wartime, 1294–1377', *Historical Research* 89 (2016): 208–26.

Maddicott, J. R., 'Parliament and the Constituencies, 1272–1377', in *The English Parliament in the Middle Ages*, ed. R. G. Davies and J. H. Denton (Manchester: Manchester University Press, 1981), 61–87.

McLeod, Glenda, '"Wholly guilty, wholly innocent": Self-definition in Héloïse's Letters to Abélard', in *Dear Sister: Medieval Women and the Epistolary Genre*, ed. Karen Cherewatuk and Ulrike Wiethaus (Philadelphia: University of Pennsylvania Press, 1993), 64–86.

McSheffrey, Shannon, 'Detective Fiction in the Archives: Court Records and the Uses of Law in Later Medieval England', *History Workshop Journal* 65 (2008): 65–78.

Musson, Anthony, 'Crossing Boundaries: Attitudes to Rape in Late Medieval England', in *The Boundaries of the Law: Geography, Gender and Jurisdiction in Medieval and Early Modern Europe*, ed. Anthony Musson (Aldershot: Ashgate, 2005), 84–101.

Musson, Anthony, *Medieval Law in Context: The Growth of Legal Consciousness from Magna Carta to the Peasants' Revolt* (Manchester: Manchester University Press, 2001).

Myers, A. R., 'Parliamentary Petitions in the Fifteenth Century', *English Historical Review* 52 (1937): 385–404, 590–613.

Ormrod, W. Mark, 'Memory, Genealogy and Nationality in Plantagenet England: The Plugenet and Walerand Estates, 1265–1368', in *Fourteenth Century England XI*, ed. David Green and Chris Given-Wilson (Woodbridge: Boydell, 2019), 77–107.

Ormrod, W. Mark, 'Murmur, Clamour and Noise: Voicing Complaint in Petitions to the English Crown, *c.* 1300–*c.* 1460', in *Medieval Petitions: Grace and Grievance*, ed. W. Mark Ormrod, Gwilym Dodd and Anthony Musson (York: York Medieval Press, 2009), 135–55.

Pollard, A. F., 'The Clerical Organisation of Parliament', *English Historical Review* 57 (1942a): 31–58.

Pollard, A. F., 'The Clerk of the Crown', *English Historical Review* 57 (1942b): 312–33.

Pollard, A. F., 'Receivers of Petitions and Clerks of Parliament', *English Historical Review* 57 (1942c): 202–26.

Ramsay, Nigel, 'Retained Legal Counsel, *c.* 1275–*c.* 1475', *Transactions of the Royal Historical Society* 5th ser. 35 (1985): 95–112.

Ramsay, Nigel, 'Scriveners and Notaries as Legal Intermediaries in Later Medieval England', in *Enterprise and Individuals in the Fifteenth Century*, ed. Jennifer I. Kermode (Gloucester: Sutton, 1991), 118–31.

Unpublished Dissertations

Bevan, Kitrina, 'Clerks and Scriveners: Legal Literacy and Access to Justice in Late Medieval England' (University of Exeter PhD thesis, 2013).

Index[1]

[1] Note: Page numbers followed by 'n' refer to notes.

W. M. Ormrod, *Women and Parliament in Later Medieval England*, The New Middle Ages,
https://doi.org/10.1007/978-3-030-45220-9

O

P

The manufacturer's authorised representative in the EU is Springer
Nature Customer Service Centre GmbH, Europaplatz 3, 69115 Heidelberg,
Germany. If you have any concerns regarding our products, please
contact ProductSafety@springernature.com

Printed and bound by CPI Group (UK) Ltd, Croydon, CR0 4YY
30/09/2026
02225609-0011